HODGES UNIVERSITY
LIBRARY - FT. MYERS

P9-CMY-570

SECOND
EDITION

(1)

Weaving It Together

Connecting Reading and Writing

MILADA BROUKAL

THOMSON
™
HEINLE

Australia • Canada • Mexico • Singapore • United Kingdom • United States

THOMSON

HEINLE

**Weaving It Together: Connecting Reading and Writing,
Book 1/Second Edition**
Milada Broukal

Publisher, Adult and Academic ESL: James W. Brown
Acquisitions Editor: Sherrise Roehr
Sr. Developmental Editor: Ingrid Wisniewska
Sr. Production Editor: Maryellen Killeen
Sr. Marketing Manager: Charlotte Sturdy
Sr. Print Buyer: Mary Beth Hennebury
Editorial Assistant: Audra Longert
Project Manager: Lifland et al., Bookmakers

Compositor: Parkwood Composition
Photography Manager: Sheri Blaney
Photo Researcher: Susan Van Etten
Illustrator: Ashley Van Etten
Cover Designer: Rotunda Design/Gina Petti
Interior Designer: Carole Rollins
Printer: Transcontinental Printing

Copyright © 2004 by Heinle, a part of the Thomson Corporation. Heinle, Thomson, and the Thomson logo are trademarks used herein under license.

Printed in Canada
8 9 10   09 08 07 06

For more information contact Heinle, 25 Thomson Place, Boston, Massachusetts 02210 USA, or you can visit our Internet site at http://www.heinle.com

All rights reserved. No part of this work covered by the copyright hereon may be reproduced or used in any form or by any means—graphic, electronic, or mechanical, including photocopying, recording, taping, Web distribution or information storage and retrieval systems—without the written permission of the publisher.

For permission to use material from this text or product contact us:
Tel   1-800-730-2214
Fax   1-800-730-2215
Web   www.thomsonrights.com

Library of Congress Cataloging-in-Publication Data

Broukal, Milada.
    Weaving it together: connecting reading and writing/Milada Broukal.
        p. cm.
    Includes bibliographical references.
    Contents: Bk. 1. Beginning level
    ISE ISBN 1413020453
    1. English language—Textbooks for foreign speakers. I. Title.

PE1128 .B7154 2003
428.2'4—dc21   2002032930

ISBN 10: 0-8384-4797-X
ISBN 13: 978-0-8384-4797-0

Photo credits: Cover: (top) Bonnie Kamin/Index Stock Imagery; (bottom) Carl Rosenstein/Index Stock Imagery. p. 1: © Zephyr Pictures/Index Stock Imagery, Inc. p. 2: © Sandy Clark/Index Stock Imagery, Inc. p. 13: © Richard A. Brooks/Getty Images. p. 27: (left) © 2002 CORBIS; (top right) © David Ball/Index Stock Imagery, Inc.; (bottom right) © 2002 CORBIS. p. 28: © Ary Diesendruck/Getty Images. p. 31: (top) © David Samuel Robbins/CORBIS; (center) © Mark Segal/Index Stock Imagery, Inc.; (bottom) © Susan Van Etten. p. 39: (left) © Mick Roessler/Index Stock Imagery, Inc.; (right) © Susan Van Etten. p. 53: © Tony Campbell/Index Stock Imagery, Inc. p. 54: © Alistair Cowin/Index Stock Imagery, Inc. p. 64: © Bettmann/CORBIS. p. 75: © Kevin Fleming/CORBIS. p. 76: (left) © Omni Photo Communications, Inc./Index Stock Imagery, Inc.; (right) © Dan Gair Photography/Index Stock Imagery, Inc. p. 88: © J. Beam Photography. p. 99: © BSIP Agency/Index Stock Imagery, Inc. p. 100: © Eric Kamp/Index Stock Imagery, Inc. p. 111: © Underwood Archives/Index Stock Imagery, Inc. p. 123: © Ewing Galloway/Index Stock Imagery, Inc. p. 124: © Jack Fields/CORBIS. p. 135: © Fulvio Roiter/CORBIS. p. 147: (left) © Reuters NewMedia, Inc./CORBIS; (top right) © Ken Goff/TimePix; (bottom right) © Flip Shulke/CORBIS. p. 148: © Duomo/CORBIS. p. 158: © AFP/CORBIS. p. 171: © Robert Ginn/Index Stock Imagery, Inc. p. 172: © Hulton Archive/Getty Images. p. 182: © CORBIS. **Text credit:** p. 173: The poem "Rain" reprinted with permission of Dionne Brand.

Brief Contents

Weaving It Together 1 Contents

Contents

To the Teacher

Rationale

Weaving It Together, Book 1, is the first in a four-book series that integrates reading and writing skills for students of English as a second or foreign language. The complete program includes the following:

Book 1—Beginning Level

Book 2—High Beginning Level

Book 3—Intermediate Level

Book 4—High Intermediate Level

The central premise of *Weaving It Together* is that reading and writing are interwoven and inextricable skills. Good readers write well; good writers read well. With this premise in mind, **Weaving It Together** has been developed to meet the following objectives:

1. To combine reading and writing through a comprehensive, systematic, and engaging process designed to integrate the two effectively.
2. To provide academically bound students with serious and engaging multicultural content.
3. To promote individualized and cooperative learning within moderate-to large-sized classes.

Over the past few years, a number of noted researchers in the field of second language acquisition have written about the serious need to integrate reading and writing instruction in both classroom practice and materials development. *Weaving It Together* is, in many ways, a response to this need.

Barbara Kroll (1993), for example, talks of teaching students to read like writers and write like readers. She notes: "It is only when a writer is able to cast himself or herself in the role of a reader of the text under preparation that he or she is able to anticipate the reader's needs by writing into the text what he or she expects or wants the reader to take out from the text." Through its systematic approach to integrating reading and writing, **Weaving It Together** teaches ESL and EFL students to understand the kinds of interconnections that they need to make between reading and writing in order to achieve academic success.

Linda Lonon Blanton's research (1992) focuses on the need for second language students to develop authority, conviction, and certainty in their writing. She believes that students develop strong writing skills in concert with good reading skills. Blanton writes: "My experience tells me that empowerment, or achieving this certainty and authority, can be achieved only through performance—through the act of speaking and writing about texts, through developing individual responses to texts." For Blanton, as for Kroll and others, both reading and writing must be treated as composing processes. Effective writing instruction must be integrally linked with effective reading instruction. This notion is at the heart of *Weaving It Together.*

Organization of the Text

Weaving It Together, Book 1, contains eight thematically organized units, each of which includes two interrelated chapters. Each chapter begins with a reading, moves on to a set of activities designed to develop critical reading skills, and culminates with a series of interactive writing exercises.

Each chapter contains the same sequence of activities:

1. **Pre-reading activity and key vocabulary:** Each chapter is introduced with a photograph, accompanied by a set of discussion questions and a vocabulary matching exercise. The purpose of the pre-reading activity is to prepare students for the reading by activating their background knowledge and encouraging them to call on and share their experiences. The purpose of the key vocabulary is to acquaint them with the words that appear in the reading. This vocabulary exercise can be done before or after the reading.

2. **Reading:** Each reading is a high-interest passage related to the theme of the unit. Selected topics include New Year's Day, Sleep, and Chocolate. The final unit contains readings from literature.

3. **Vocabulary:** Six to eight key vocabulary words or phrases appear in bold type in each reading passage. In the vocabulary exercises that follow the passage, students practice using these words. There are two types of vocabulary exercises. The first one, *Meaning,* uses the new words in the context in which they were used in the reading. The second one, *Vocabulary Activity,* helps students to use the words in new contexts. The vocabulary items then serve as a useful resource for students when they are writing their own sentences on the same theme.

4. **Comprehension:** There are two types of comprehension exercises. The first, *Looking for the Main Ideas,* concentrates on a general understanding of the reading. This exercise may be done after a first silent reading of the text. Students can reread the text to check answers. The second comprehension exercise, *Looking for Details,* concentrates on developing skimming and scanning skills.

5. **Discussion:** Working in small or large groups, students are encouraged to interact with one another to discuss questions that arise from the reading. The discussion questions ask students to relate their experiences to what they have learned from the reading.

6. **Writing skills:** Following each of the sixteen readings, a different aspect of writing at the sentence level is presented. These aspects include sentence word order, capitalization and punctuation, and the use of adjectives, adverbs, and prepositions. Exercises on the points taught provide reinforcement.

7. **Writing practice:** Students are asked to write a paragraph, using the ideas they have generated in the discussion section and the grammar points they have practiced. The text takes them through the writing process one step at a time. First they write sentences about themselves, in answer to questions presented in the text. Next students rewrite their sentences in the form of a paragraph, using a checklist (on their own or with a partner) to check their paragraphs and then making any necessary alterations. Teachers are encouraged to add to the checklist provided any further points they consider important. In the third step, students are encouraged to work with a partner or their teacher to correct spelling, punctuation, vocabulary, and grammar. Finally, students prepare the final version of their paragraphs.

Optional Expansion Activities

1. **Quiz:** At the end of each unit is a fun quiz related to the theme of the unit. The answers appear at the end of the book. The quiz questions are meant to be a light-hearted way to end the unit. Use them as a team competition or as a game. Students can also make up further quiz questions to test each other.

2. **Video activity:** Following the quiz is a video activity related to the CNN videotapes that accompany this series. The video activity can be used to expand vocabulary and themes in the unit. Each video activity ends with a discussion question, which can be used as a springboard for further writing.

To the Teacher

3. **Internet activity:** Also at the end of each unit is an Internet activity, which gives students the opportunity to develop their Internet research skills. This activity may be done in a classroom setting, under the guidance of the teacher, or—if students have Internet access—as a homework task leading to a classroom presentation or discussion. Each internet activity has two parts. The first part involves doing some research on the Internet using the key words suggested. The second part involves evaluating web sites in order to assess the reliability of the information they contain.

Journal Writing

In addition to doing the projects and exercises in the book, I strongly recommend that students be instructed to keep a journal in which they correspond with you. The purpose of this journal is for them to tell you how they feel about the class each day. It gives them an opportunity to tell you what they like, what they dislike, what they understand, and what they don't understand. By having students explain what they have learned in the class, you can discover whether they understand the concepts taught.

Journal writing is effective for two major reasons. First, because this type of writing focuses on fluency and personal expression, students always have something to write about. Second, journal writing can be used to identify language concerns and trouble spots that need further review. In its finest form, journal writing becomes an active dialogue between teacher and student that permits you to learn more about your students' lives and to individualize their language instruction.

References

Blanton, Linda Lonon. 1992. "Reading, Writing, and Authority: Issues in Developmental ESL." *College ESL,* 2, 11–19.

Kroll, Barbara. 1993. "Teaching Writing *Is* Teaching Reading: Training the New Teacher of ESL Composition." In *Reading in the Composition Classroom.* Boston: Heinle & Heinle Publishers, pp. 61-81.

To the Student

This book will teach you to read and write in English. You will study readings on selected themes and learn strategies for writing good sentences on those themes. In the process, you will learn to express your own ideas in sentences and work toward writing a paragraph in good English.

It is important for you to know that writing well in English may be quite different from writing well in your native language. Good Chinese, Arabic, or Spanish writing is different from good English writing. Not only are the styles different, but the organization is different too.

The processes of reading and writing are closely interconnected. Therefore, in this book, we are weaving reading and writing together. I hope that the readings in the book will stimulate your interest to write and that *Weaving It Together* will make writing in English much easier for you.

Note for the New Edition

In this new edition of *Weaving It Together, Book 1*, the readings are longer, and I have added extra vocabulary exercises. There is a new unit with readings from literature. For those of you who enjoy using different media, I have also added CNN video and Internet activities. I hope that you will enjoy using these new features and that *Weaving It Together* will continue to help you toward success.

Special Days

CHAPTER ONE

Birthdays

Pre-Reading Activity

Discuss these questions.

1. What do you see in the picture?
2. How is the birthday in the picture different from a birthday in your country?
3. Do you like birthdays? Why or why not?

Key Vocabulary

Do you know these words? Match the words with the meanings.

1. ____ to celebrate
2. ____ customs
3. ____ to gather around
4. ____ one breath
5. ____ a flag
6. ____ flavors
7. ____ lucky

a. the habits of a country or group
b. to do something special and fun for a reason
c. helping good things happen by chance
d. a piece of cloth with special colors for a country
e. to stand together in a group
f. special tastes
g. the amount of air that you take into your body and then let out again

Birthdays

Everybody has a birthday. Many children in other countries **celebrate** their birthdays like children in the United States. They have a birthday cake, gifts, and sometimes a birthday party for friends. Friends and family **gather around** a table with a birthday cake on it. They sing "Happy Birthday to You." Two American sisters wrote this song in 1893, but people still sing this song today! The birthday cake usually has lighted candles on it, one candle for each year of your life. The birthday child makes a wish and then blows out all the candles. If the child blows out the candles in **one breath**, the wish will come true. Other countries have different **customs.**

In Norway, Denmark, and Sweden, people fly the country's **flag** outside their home to tell everyone that someone in the family is having a birthday. In Denmark, a parent puts gifts around a child's bed when the child is sleeping at night. When the child wakes up in the morning, the gifts will be the first thing the child sees. In Sweden and also in Finland, the birthday child gets breakfast in bed!

In some countries, some years are more important than others. In Holland, these are 5, 10, 15, 20, and 21.They call them "crown" years. On a crown birthday, the birthday child gets a much more important gift. The family also decorates the child's chair at the dining table with flowers, paper, and balloons. The special years in Japan are 3, 5, and 7. These are the **lucky** years. On November 15 every year, there is a festival called "Seven, five, three" when the children and their families go to a religious place. Then the family gives a party for the child and gives the child gifts. Because of religious reasons, Hindu children only get to celebrate their birthdays until the age of sixteen.

Birthday cakes around the world come in different sizes and **flavors.** There are even ice cream birthday cakes today. In China, there is no birthday cake. Friends and family go out to lunch, and to wish the birthday child a long life they eat noodles!

Vocabulary

Meaning

Complete the sentences. Circle the letter of the correct answer.

1. Children in the United States _____ their birthday with a cake, gifts, and a birthday party.
   a. celebrate
   b. say

2. People around the world have different birthday _____.
   a. customs
   b. countries

3. Friends and family _____ the child and the birthday cake.
   a. blow out
   b. gather around

4. It is sometimes not easy to blow out the candles in one _____.
   a. wish
   b. breath

5. In Norway, Sweden, and Denmark, people put a _____ outside the house.
   a. flag
   b. gift

6. Birthday cakes can have a chocolate _____.
   a. flavor
   b. noodle

7. In Japan, 3, 5, and 7 are _____ years.
   a. happy
   b. lucky

Vocabulary Activity

Answer the questions. Use complete sentences.

1. What color is the flag of your country?

    Example: _The flag of my country is red, white, and blue._

    _____

    _____

2. What other days do people celebrate?

    _____

    _____

3. What is your favorite flavor of ice cream?

    _____

    _____

4. What is a birthday custom in your country?

    _____

    _____

Comprehension

Looking for the Main Ideas

Read the passage again and look for the MAIN IDEAS. Circle the letter of the best answer.

1. Children in other countries celebrate birthdays _____.
   a. like people in the United States
   b. with just their friends
   c. in different ways

2. In Norway, Denmark, and Sweden, people _____ on a child's birthday.
   a. fly a flag
   b. have breakfast in bed
   c. put gifts in the child's bed

3. In some countries, some _____ are more important than others.
   a. cakes
   b. years
   c. festivals

4. Birthday cakes _____.
   a. are the same around the world
   b. have noodles in China
   c. are different everywhere

Looking for Details

Read the passage again and look for DETAILS. Circle T if the sentence is true. Circle F if the sentence is false.

1. There is one candle on a birthday cake.   T   F

2. In Denmark, they put gifts around the birthday cake.   T   F

3. Two sisters wrote the famous birthday song.   T   F

4. The crown years are 5, 10, 15, 20, and 21.   T   F

5. In Finland, the child eats breakfast in bed.   T   F

6. Hindu children celebrate their birthday after age sixteen.   T   F

Discussion

Discuss these questions with your classmates.

1. Which birthday custom in the reading do you like best? Why?
2. How do you usually celebrate a birthday in your country?
3. Are birthdays important in your country? Is another day, such as your name day or New Year's Day, more important?
4. Do you celebrate your birthday every year or only in special years?

A sentence always has a subject and a verb. Many sentences also have an object. The sentence order in English is usually as follows:

Example:

subject	verb	object
John	has	a birthday.
(Subject)	(Verb)	(Object)

The Subject

The *subject* is usually a noun, a pronoun, or a phrase with a noun. It tells us who is doing the action and usually comes before the verb. Look at the subjects in the following sentences:

Examples:

John has a birthday.
(The subject is a noun.)

He has a birthday.
(The subject is a pronoun.)

The tall boy has a birthday.
(The subject is a phrase with a noun.)

The tall boy with black hair has a birthday.
(The prepositional phrase **with black hair** comes after the noun and is part of the whole subject.)

Underline the subject in each sentence.

1. She has a brother.

2. Mary Peel loves children.

3. The tall woman has a birthday today.

4. The tall woman with white hair has a birthday today.

5. Many children have a birthday cake.

6. Birthday cakes are a custom.

7. Customs in some countries are strange.

8. Parents in Denmark put gifts around the birthday child's bed.

The Verb

The *verb* tells us the action of the subject. Some verbs are one word, but other verbs are more than one word.

Examples:

Mary has a birthday today.
    (Verb)

Mary is having a birthday.
    (Verb)

Mary is going to have a birthday tomorrow.
    (Verb)

Underline the subject with one line and the verb with two lines in the following sentences.

1. She has many gifts.

2. The child cries.

3. The little girl is crying.

4. The little girl with the red hair is going to cry.

5. Many friends are going to say happy birthday.

Punctuation and Capitalization

A sentence always begins with a capital letter and ends with either a period (.), an exclamation point (!), or a question mark (?). The first word after a comma (,) begins with a small letter.

Here are some rules for using capital letters.

Capitalization Rules

1. Capitalize the first word in a sentence.
   Many children have a birthday cake on their birthday.

2. Capitalize the pronoun *I.*
   John and I have the same birthday.

3. Capitalize all proper nouns. Here are some proper nouns:
   a. Names of people and their titles:

Mr. John Sands	Ms. Mary Lee
Robert	Diana
Bob Briggs	Chan Lai Fong

   b. Names of cities, states, and countries:

London, England	Houston, Texas
Acapulco	Hong Kong
Taiwan	Korea

c. Names of days and months:

Monday	Saturday
May	July
Friday	August

Exercise 3

Change the small letters to capital letters where necessary.

1. maria is from mexico city, mexico.

2. victor is from lima, peru.

3. ito and mayumi are from tokyo, japan.

4. the test is on monday, october 7.

5. mohammed's birthday is on tuesday, april 10th.

6. wednesday, june 5th, is bob's birthday.

7. my sister suzie and i were born in february.

8. mrs. lee's birthday is in december.

9. mr. brown and i are going to a party on friday.

10. i am going to milan, italy, in july.

Exercise 4

Find the mistakes. There are 10 mistakes in grammar and capitalization. Find and correct them.

My birthday is on june 11. I was born in lima, peru. We has a party on my Birthday. My friends comes. My mother make a cake. I get many gift. I always happy on my birthday. It is my special Day.

Writing Practice

1. Write sentences.

   Answer these questions with complete sentences. Use capital letters and periods where necessary.

   a. What is your full name?

   _____

   _____

   b. Where do you come from? (Give the city and country.)

   _____

   _____

   c. When is your birthday?

   _____

   _____

   d. What is the full name of a student in your class?

   _____

   _____

   e. Where does he or she come from? (Give the city and country.)

   _____

   _____

   f. When is his or her birthday?

   _____

   _____

   g. What do you usually do on your birthday (have a birthday cake, have a party, go out)?

   _____

   _____

New Year's Day

Pre-Reading Activity

Discuss these questions.

1. When do you celebrate the New Year in your country?
2. What kinds of food do you eat on New Year's Eve or New Year's Day?
3. Do you go out or do you stay at home for the New Year celebration?
4. What are three things most people do on New Year's Eve or New Year's Day?

Key Vocabulary

Do you know these words? Match the words with the meanings.

1. ____ extra   a. what you walk on
2. ____ to bow   b. with nobody or nothing in it
3. ____ ground   c. the part of the face above the eyes and below the hair
4. ____ forehead   d. members of your family
5. ____ empty   e. showing good manners
6. ____ polite   f. more than needed
7. ____ relatives   g. to lower your head to show respect

New Year's Day

The Chinese New Year is the most important holiday for the Chinese people. For the Chinese, the New Year comes on the first day of the First Moon, between January 21 and February 19.

One week before the New Year, people start to clean their homes and buy new things. Some people paint their homes for the New Year. They buy new pictures, too. New Year's pictures often have oranges in them. In Chinese, the word for "oranges" sounds the same as the word for "gold." It is a lucky word. People buy new clothes for the New Year. It is important to start the New Year in new clothes.

On New Year's Eve, the family gets together to eat a big meal. The meal starts late in the afternoon of New Year's Eve. There are many special dishes on the table. There are usually oranges and a dish of fish. Every family tries to eat fish. At the end of the meal, they leave some **extra** fish on the plate to bring good luck.

The New Year is an important time for the family. It is a tradition for the younger people to **bow** to the older people. The Chinese call this k'ou t'ou or kowtow. This means "to touch the **ground** with the **forehead**." Then the older people give children gifts of money in red envelopes. Red is a lucky color for the Chinese.

At midnight, there are fireworks. It is New Year's Day or the first day of the First Moon, Yuan Tuan. In the morning, the shops are closed, and the streets are **empty**. People dress in their new clothes and try to be kind and **polite** to each other to start the New Year well. Later, they go to visit their friends and **relatives**.

Vocabulary

Meaning

Complete the sentences. Circle the letter of the correct answer.

1. At dinner, the Chinese leave some _____ fish on their plate.
    a. extra
    b. orange

2. Young people usually _____ to older people in China.
    a. give
    b. bow

3. When people bow, they lower their _____.
    a. forehead
    b. foot

4. In China, many people touch the _____ when they bow.
    a. ground
    b. picture

5. People are _____ to each other to start the New Year well.
    a. happy
    b. polite

6. People visit their _____ in the New Year.
    a. sisters
    b. relatives

7. In the morning of the first day of the New Year, the streets are
    _____.

    a. important
    b. empty

Vocabulary Activity

Work with a partner. Read the questions and add the letters to complete the answers.

1. What is the name of this **relative:** your father's brother?

   __ N__ __ E

2. What is a **polite** word in English?

   P L __ A __ __

3. If your glass is **empty,** what is in it?

   __ __ T H __ N G

4. What do you have under your **forehead?**

   __ Y__ B __ __ __ S

Now make a sentence with each of the words in bold.

Example: My uncle Armando is my favorite relative.

Comprehension

Looking for the Main Ideas

Write complete answers to these questions.

1. What is the most important holiday for Chinese people?

    _____

    _____

2. What do people do one week before the New Year?

    _____

    _____

3. For whom is the New Year an important time?

    _____

    _____

Looking for Details

One word in each sentence is not correct. Rewrite the sentence with the correct word.

1. The Chinese New Year comes on the first day of the First Year, between January 21 and February 19.

    _____

    _____

2. New Year's pictures often have family in them.

    _____

    _____

3. It is important to start the New Year in new homes.

    _____

    _____

4. Every family tries to eat meat.

_____

_____

5. The older people give children gifts of clothes in red envelopes.

_____

_____

6. At the end of the meal, people leave some oranges on the plate.

_____

_____

Discussion

Discuss these questions with your classmates.

1. Are any of the New Year's customs in the reading the same as customs in your country?
2. What do people wear for the New Year in your country?
3. Do people decorate their homes or shops?
4. Do people give or get gifts on this day?
5. How is the American celebration of the New Year different from the celebration in your country (as far as you know)?

Sentence Order

As you know from Chapter 1, sentence order in English is usually as follows:

  subject   verb   object

The *verb* does the action. The *subject* tells us who is doing the action. The *object* answers the question "What?"

The Object

The object can be a *noun,* a *pronoun,* or a *noun phrase.*

Examples:

  <u>People</u>   <u>buy</u>   <u>new pictures.</u>
  (Subject)   (Verb)   (Object)

  <u>Older people</u>   <u>give</u>   <u>gifts of money.</u>
  (Subject)   (Verb)   (Object)

The Complement

Some verbs are not action verbs; they are linking verbs. Some examples are *like, be, become, seem,* and *feel.* These verbs may be followed by a noun, a noun phrase, or an adjective. This is called a *complement.*

Examples:

  <u>The streets</u>   <u>are</u>   <u>empty.</u>
  (Subject)   (Verb)   (Complement)

  <u>The color red</u>   <u>is</u>   <u>good luck.</u>
  (Subject)   (Verb)   (Complement)

Underline the object or the complement in each sentence.

1. People close the shops.

2. Some people paint their homes.

3. The older people give red envelopes.

4. The Chinese New Year is important.

5. Our family prepares special food.

6. People wear their best clothes.

7. Many people visit relatives.

8. Relatives bring many gifts.

Punctuation and Capitalization

Remember that a sentence always begins with a capital letter and ends with a period (.), an exclamation point (!), or a question mark (?). Here are some more rules for using capital letters.

Capitalization Rules

1. Capitalize names of nationalities, races, languages, and religions.

American	Chinese
Muslim	Catholic
Hispanic	Asian
Italian	Arab

2. Capitalize names of special days.

New Year's Day	Independence Day
Christmas	Halloween

Exercise 2

Change the small letters to capital letters where necessary.

1. we do not have classes during christmas and easter vacation.

2. on new year's day, we stay at home.

3. the american woman celebrated chinese new year with us.

4. in our class, we have students who are buddhist, muslim, christian, and jewish.

5. for us, new year's day is more important than christmas.

6. all over the united states on july 4, americans celebrate independence day.

Exercise 3

Find the mistakes. There are 10 mistakes in grammar and capitalization. Find and correct them.

Pat and Don hutton live in boston, in the united states. They are americans. They are also christian. They celebrates christmas on december 25. It an important holiday for them.

Writing Practice

1. Write sentences.

   Answer these questions with complete sentences. Use capital letters and periods where necessary.

   a. What is the most important holiday in your country?

   _____

   _____

   b. When do you celebrate it?

   _____

   _____

   c. What do you wear on this holiday?

   _____

   _____

   d. Where do you go?

   _____

   _____

   e. What food do you prepare or eat?

   _____

   _____

   f. Do you give or get gifts?

   _____

   _____

   g. Why is this holiday important?

   _____

   _____

2. Rewrite in paragraph form.

Rewrite your sentences in the form of a paragraph like the one below.

Paragraph Form

It is important that you start to write using the form of a paragraph. In *Weaving It Together, Book 2,* you will learn how to write a good paragraph with a topic sentence. But for now it is important for you just to follow the format.

1. Use lined paper.
2. Write your name, the date, and the course number in the upper right-hand corner of the paper.
3. Write a title in the center at the top of the page. Capitalize the first word, last word, and all important words in the title. Do not capitalize *the, a, an,* or prepositions unless they begin the title.
4. Leave a 1-inch margin on the left-hand side of the page. (Your teacher may ask you to leave a margin on the right-hand side also.)
5. Indent the first line of every paragraph.
6. Write on every other line of the paper.
7. Capitalize the first word in each sentence and end each sentence with a period.

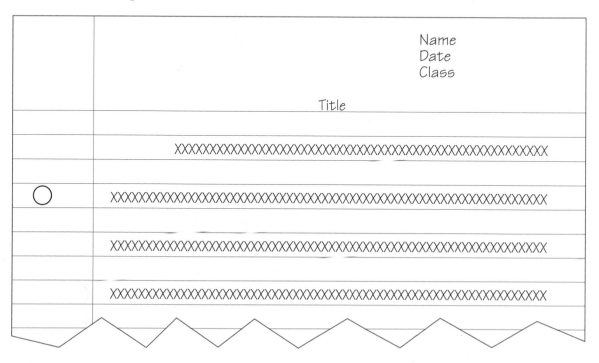

The list below will help you check your paragraph form:

Checklist

_____ Did you indent the first line?

_____ Did you give your paragraph a title?

_____ Did you write the title with a capital letter?

_____ Did you put the title in the center at the top of the page?

_____ Did you write on every other line?

3. Edit your work.

   Work with a partner or your teacher to edit your sentences. Correct spelling, punctuation, vocabulary, and grammar.

4. Write your final copy.

Do you know these interesting facts about special days?

Circle T if the sentence is true. Circle F if the sentence is false.

1. On New Year's Day in Madagascar, everyone pours water over each other.   T   F

2. Ten million people have the same birthday as you.   T   F

3. Canadians celebrate Thanksgiving on the same day as people in the United States.   T   F

4. The British celebrate Thanksgiving on the fourth Thursday in November.   T   F

5. In early May in Japan, men fly kites to celebrate the birth of their first-born sons.   T   F

6. Father's Day is an official holiday in the United States.   T   F

7. The British celebrate Independence Day on July 4.   T   F

8. At an American wedding, people throw rice at the bride.   T   F

Video Activity • Birthdays and Birthday Parties CNN

1. People celebrate birthdays in different ways. Which of these things do you expect to see at a birthday celebration?

    ☐ gifts   ☐ flowers   ☐ cake
    ☐ candles   ☐ singing   ☐ laughing
    ☐ balloons   ☐ pizza   ☐ crying
    ☐ dancing   ☐ fruit   ☐ family

2. Now watch the video. Which of these things did you see? What other things did you see that are connected to birthday celebrations?

3. How are the birthday celebrations in the video different from your birthday celebrations when you were a child?

Internet Activity

The New Year is celebrated on different days in different cultures. Go to the Internet to find out more about New Year's customs around the world. When is the next Chinese New Year, Jewish New Year, Iranian New Year, and Muslim New Year?

Places

CHAPTER THREE

Brasilia

Pre-Reading Activity

Discuss these questions.

1. What capital cities do you know in South America?
2. Do you like modern cities or old cities?
3. What city do you think is great? Why?

Key Vocabulary

Do you know these words? Match the words with the meanings.

1. _____ an architect
2. _____ a cathedral
3. _____ in the shape of
4. _____ high-rises
5. _____ extraordinary
6. _____ slums

a. wonderful, unusual, not ordinary
b. tall buildings
c. a person who makes plans for buildings
d. a main church of an area
e. part of a city where poor people live in bad housing
f. with the same form or outline as

Brasilia

When we think of Brazil, we think of Rio de Janeiro. But the capital of Brazil is not Rio de Janeiro. It is Brasilia. Brasilia is a new city in the center of Brazil. It is 600 miles from the Atlantic Ocean and far away from any other town.

For a long time, Brazilians wanted to have a capital in the center of the country. They wanted people to live in the center and not just by the ocean. In 1957, President Kubitschek decided to build the city. Workers came from all over the country. There were no roads or railroads to the center of the country. Everything came by plane. It took three years to build this city. In 1960, Brasilia became the capital.

The city is **in the shape of** an airplane. The government buildings are in the center. People live in apartments in **high-rises** on both sides. There are wide boulevards and modern buildings. The main buildings and the **cathedral** are the work of Oscar Niemeyer. He is a famous **architect.** The cathedral is **extraordinary.**

Brasilia has problems as a city. The city was made for half a million people. Now about two million people live in Brasilia. The poor people live in **slums** outside the city, like in other Brazilian cities. It is hot in the center of Brazil, and there are few trees in the new city. There aren't too many people outside in the streets. Some of the streets are very wide. They are really for cars. It is not easy for people to cross the streets.

Brasilia is a very modern capital. It is a beautiful city. It has everything a city needs. But many people miss the exciting life in Rio de Janeiro and often go back there.

Vocabulary

Meaning

Complete the sentences. Circle the letter of the correct answer.

1. Architects made Brasilia ——————— an airplane.
   a. in the center of
   b. in the shape of

2. There are many ——————— where people live.
   a. high-rises
   b. government buildings

3. Oscar Niemeyer is a famous ———————.
   a. boulevard
   b. architect

4. Niemeyer made the plans for a very special ———————.
   a. cathedral
   b. city

5. People say the very modern cathedral is ———————.
   a. poor
   b. extraordinary

6. Poor people live outside Brasilia in ———————.
   a. slums
   b. cars

Vocabulary Activity

Use the words below to make sentences about the pictures.

cathedral   high-rise(s)
in the shape of   extraordinary

1.

Example:

<u>The cathedral in Barcelona is in the shape of a crown.</u>

_____

_____

_____

_____

Sagrada Familia Cathedral, Barcelona

2.

_____

_____

_____

_____

Sears Tower, Chicago

3.

_____

_____

_____

_____

TransAmerican Building, San Francisco

Comprehension

Looking for the Main Ideas

Circle the letter of the best answer.

1. The capital of Brazil —————.
    a. is not in the center of Brazil
    b. is Rio de Janeiro
    c. is a new city

2. The city —————.
    a. has airplanes
    b. has a modern cathedral
    c. is like an airplane

3. Brasilia —————.
    a. is not a beautiful city
    b. has problems
    c. is a city for poor people

Looking for Details

One word in each sentence is not correct. Rewrite the sentence with the correct word.

1. Brasilia is a new country in the center of Brazil.

    _____

    _____

2. About half a million people live in Brasilia today.

    _____

    _____

3. Oscar Niemeyer is a famous president.

    _____

    _____

4. It took thirty years to build the capital.

_____

_____

5. The cathedral buildings are in the center.

_____

_____

6. It is hot in the center of Brazil, and there are few people in the new city.

_____

_____

Discussion

Discuss these questions with your classmates.

1. Is your city like Brasilia? How is it different or similar?
2. Describe a special place (for example, a building or a park) in the city where you are now.
3. Describe a special place in another city or town you know.
4. What city or place do you want to visit one day? Why?

Adjectives

Words that describe nouns are called *adjectives.* They usually answer the question "What kind?"

Examples:

Brasilia is a   <u>new</u>   <u>city.</u>
            (Adjective)   (Noun)

He is a   <u>famous</u>   <u>architect.</u>
           (Adjective)   (Noun)

Adjectives are the same with a singular noun or a plural noun.

Examples:

There are   <u>wide</u>   <u>boulevards.</u>
           (Adjective)   (Plural noun)

There are   <u>modern</u>   <u>buildings.</u>
           (Adjective)   (Plural noun)

Adjectives come before nouns.

Examples:

Brasilia is a **modern** city.
The **government** buildings are in the center.

Adjectives can also come after a form of the verb *to be.*

Examples:

It is **hot** in the center of Brazil.
The cathedral is **extraordinary**.

Exercise 1

Underline the adjectives in the sentences.

1. The main buildings are in the center.

2. People live in modern high-rises.

3. The famous cathedral is the work of Oscar Niemeyer.

4. The streets are wide.

5. The poor people live in slums.

Exercise 2

Put the words in the correct order.

1. Brasilia / city / is / a / modern

    Example: _Brasilia is a modern city._

2. Oscar Niemeyer / architect / is / famous / a

    _____

    _____

3. In 1960, / became / the capital / Brasilia

    _____

    _____

4. The / buildings / government / in the center / are

    _____

    _____

Write about what you think. Use complete sentences. Use an adjective in each sentence.

1. What is the town you are living in now like?

   _____

   _____

2. Describe a special place in your town.

   _____

   _____

3. What is your school like?

   _____

   _____

4. What is your class like?

   _____

   _____

Find the mistakes. There are 10 mistakes in grammar and capitalization. Find and correct them.

Brazil is a big country in south america. it's capital is brasilia. This is a city new. It has moderns buildings and streets wide. About two Million people lives in this city today.

Writing Practice

1. Write sentences.

    Answer these questions with complete sentences.

    a. Name a city that is special to you.

    _____

    _____

    b. Where is this city?

    _____

    _____

    c. Describe this city using one or two adjectives.

    _____

    _____

    d. Name one thing this city has that is special. Describe it using adjectives.

    _____

    _____

    e. Name and describe a special building in this city.

    _____

    _____

2. **Rewrite in paragraph form.**

   Rewrite your sentences in the form of a paragraph (see page 23). Then check the checklist.

   Checklist

   _____ Did you indent the first line?
   _____ Did you give your paragraph a title? (Use the name of the city.)
   _____ Did you write the title with a capital letter?
   _____ Did you put the title in the center at the top of the page?
   _____ Did you write on every other line?

3. **Edit your work.**

   Work with a partner or your teacher to edit your sentences. Check spelling, punctuation, vocabulary, and grammar.

4. **Write your final copy.**

CHAPTER FOUR

Iceland

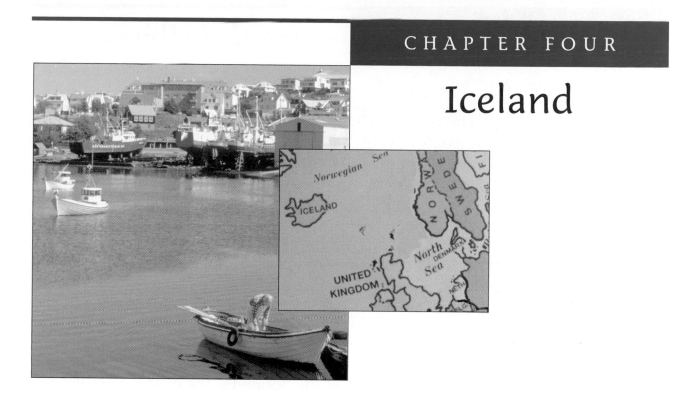

Pre-Reading Activity

Discuss these questions.

1. Where is Iceland?
2. Is it part of Europe?
3. What do you know about life in Iceland?

Key Vocabulary

Do you know these words? Match the words with the meanings.

1. ___ an island
2. ___ a quarter of
3. ___ similar to
4. ___ to heat
5. ___ crime
6. ___ a high quality of life

a. 1/4 or 25% of
b. like but not exactly the same as
c. land with water all around it
d. something people may go to prison for
e. very good way of living
f. to make hot

Iceland is **an island** in the North Atlantic Ocean. It is near Greenland and Norway, but it is part of Europe. This country has a population of about **a quarter of** a million people. Most of the people live in towns. Reykjavik is the capital and the largest city.

Iceland is not as cold as its name sounds. The temperature in January in Reykjavik is the same as in New York City. Icelanders speak Icelandic, which is **similar to** German, but 99% of Icelanders also speak English.

Icelanders are the hardest workers in Europe. They work the longest hours. Many people have two or three jobs, and children work during school vacations. Icelanders work hard because life is very expensive and they want **a high quality of life.** Iceland is the most expensive country in Europe. Iceland has a lot of fish, but it doesn't make cars or machines. Many of these things come from other countries. That is why they are expensive.

Icelanders have a great system for health and education. Health care and education are free. All children must go to school from age 6 to age 16. Every person in Iceland can read and write. Icelanders read a lot. Icelanders read more books than any other people in the world. Icelanders are healthy too. The air is clean in Iceland because people get natural hot water from the ground to **heat** their homes. With clean air and a good health system, Icelanders live long lives. Both men and women in Iceland live the longest lives of any people in the world.

Iceland is a great country. The air is clean. People live long. There's almost no **crime.** Icelanders have a high quality of life, but they work hard!

Vocabulary

Meaning

Complete the sentences. Circle the letter of the correct answer.

1. Iceland is _____, but it is also a country.
   a. an island
   b. a capital

2. About _____ a million people live in Iceland.
   a. a quarter of
   b. a population of

3. Iceland's language is _____ German.
   a. the same as
   b. similar to

4. In Iceland, people use hot water from the ground to _____ their homes.
   a. heat
   b. wash

5. There are few people in prison in Iceland because there is almost no _____.
   a. education
   b. crime

6. Icelanders like a _____ quality of life.
   a. hard
   b. high

Vocabulary Activity

Answer the questions. Use complete sentences.

1. Name a crime.

   _____

   _____

2. Name something that is important for a high quality of life.

   _____

   _____

3. Name something that people use to heat their homes.

   _____

   _____

4. Name an island.

   _____

   _____

Comprehension

Looking for the Main Ideas

Write complete answers to these questions.

1. Where is Iceland?

   _____

   _____

2. Who are the hardest workers in Europe?

   _____

   _____

3. What kind of health and education system does Iceland have?

   _____

   _____

Looking for Details

Circle T if the sentence is true. Circle F if the sentence is false.

1. In January, Reykjavik is colder than New York City.   T   F

2. The language of Iceland is English.   T   F

3. Icelanders get their hot water from the ground.   T   F

4. Fish is expensive in Iceland.   T   F

5. Icelanders read a lot of books.   T   F

6. Children in Iceland work during school vacations.   T   F

Discussion

Find students in your class who are not from your country. Then complete the chart below with information about their countries.

Country	Population	Name of Capital	Language	Special Things (foods/plants)
Iceland	1/4 of a million	Reykjavik	Icelandic	fish

Now choose a country from your chart. Use these questions to talk about it with your classmates.

1. What can you say about the capital of the country?
2. What plants or animals does the country have a lot of?
3. What other special things does the country have?

Comparing Things

The Comparative Form of Adjectives

When you compare two things that are different, use the comparative form of adjectives.

To form the comparative, add **-er** to the adjective and put **than** after the adjective.

Examples:

Iceland is **colder than** Mexico.

Mexico's population is **bigger than** the population of Iceland.

Notes:

If the adjective ends in one consonant and there is one vowel before it, double the consonant.

big, bigger   hot, hotter

If the adjective ends in **-e**, add **r.**

wide, wider   fine, finer

If the adjective ends in **-y**, change **y** to **i** and add **-er.**

happy, happier   easy, easier

When the adjective has more than two syllables, put **more** in front of the adjective and **than** after the adjective.

Examples:

Reykjavik is **more expensive than** Paris.

Paris is **more crowded than** Reykjavik.

Give the number of syllables in each adjective. Then write the comparative form.

Adjective	Syllables	Comparative Form
1. beautiful	3	more beautiful than
2. wet		
3. dry		
4. expensive		
5. old		
6. dangerous		
7. high		
8. large		

Exercise 2

Complete each sentence with the comparative form of the adjective in parentheses.

1. Iceland is (big) Switzerland.

   _____

   _____

2. Iceland is (small) Greenland.

   _____

   _____

3. The Pacific Ocean is (large) the Atlantic Ocean.

   _____

   _____

4. The Sears Tower in Chicago is (tall) the Empire State Building.

   _____

   _____

5. The Nile River is (long) the Mississippi.

_____

_____

6. Mexico is (dry) Canada.

_____

_____

7. The Taj Mahal is (beautiful) the Sears Tower.

_____

_____

8. Reykjavik is (expensive) Paris.

_____

_____

The Superlative Form of Adjectives

When you compare more than two things, use the superlative form of adjectives.

To form the superlative, add **-est** to the end of the adjective.

Examples:

Reykjavik is the **largest** city in Iceland.
Icelanders are the **hardest** workers in Europe.

When the adjective has more than two syllables, add **the most** in front of the adjective.

Examples:

Reykjavik is **the most expensive** city in Europe.
Reykjavik is **the most popular** city in Iceland.

Complete each sentence with the superlative form of the adjective in parentheses.

1. Iceland has (small) population for its size in Europe.

   _____

   _____

2. Alaska is (big) state in the United States.

   _____

   _____

3. Vatican City is (small) country in the world.

   _____

   _____

4. Mount Everest is (high) mountain in the world.

   _____

   _____

5. The Nile is (long) river in the world.

   _____

   _____

6. Death Valley in California is (hot) place in the United States.

   _____

   _____

7. Tokyo is one of (expensive) cities in the world.

   _____

   _____

8. Acapulco is (popular) city in Mexico for tourists.

   _____

   _____

Write about what you think. Use complete sentences.

1. Which is the most interesting city for you?

   _____

   _____

2. Which is the most dangerous place?

   _____

   _____

3. Which is the most beautiful place?

   _____

   _____

4. Which is the largest city in your country?

   _____

   _____

Exercise 5

Find the mistakes. There are 10 mistakes in grammar and capitalization. Find and correct them.

inga stefansson is from iceland. Iceland is a country in europe. She speak icelandic. This language is similar to german. Life in iceland is the expensivest in Europe. But people are healthy, and they live the most long lives.

Writing Practice

1. Write sentences.

   Answer these questions with complete sentences.

   a. Which country do you come from?

   _____

   _____

   b. Where is your country? (Give names of countries near your country.)

   _____

   _____

   c. What is the population of your country?

   _____

   _____

   d. What language or languages do most people in your country speak?

   _____

   _____

   e. What is the capital city of your country? Is it also the largest city? (If not, tell which city is the largest.)

   _____

   _____

   f. What special things does your country have? (Name plants, foods, animals, historic places, or natural beauty.)

   _____

   _____

g. What can you say about your country, using a superlative adjective?

Example: <u>My country is the most beautiful country in the world.</u>

_____

_____

2. Rewrite in paragraph form.

Rewrite your sentences in the form of a paragraph. Then check the checklist.

Checklist
_____ Did you indent the first line?
_____ Did you give your paragraph a title?
_____ Did you write the title with a capital letter?
_____ Did you put the title in the center at the top of the page?
_____ Did you write on every other line?

3. Edit your work.

Work with a partner or your teacher to edit your sentences. Correct spelling, punctuation, vocabulary, and grammar.

4. Write your final copy.

Do you know these interesting facts about places?

Circle the correct answer.

1. The largest city in the world in area is _____.
   a. London, England
   b. New York City, United States
   c. Mount Isa, Australia

2. The oldest capital city in the world is _____.
   a. Rome, Italy
   b. Damascus, Syria
   c. Athens, Greece

3. The world's largest palace is _____.
   a. the Imperial Palace, Beijing, China
   b. Versailles, France
   c. Buckingham Palace, London, England

4. The South Pole is _____.
   a. warmer than the North Pole
   b. colder than the North Pole
   c. the same temperature as the North Pole

5. The highest and lowest points in the United States are both in the state of _____.
   a. California
   b. Colorado
   c. Arizona

6. The name "El Pueblo de Nuestra Señora la Reina de los Angeles de Porciuncola" was the original name of _____.
   a. California
   b. the cathedral in Mexico City
   c. Los Angeles

Video Activity • A Visit to Costa Rica

CNN

1. What do you know about Costa Rica? Where is it? What do you think it is like in Costa Rica? Discuss each of these topics:

    a. geography   d. religion

    b. people   e. weather

    c. language   f. places to stay

2. Now watch the video. Write key words for each topic. Then compare your notes with a partner.

3. Would you like to visit Costa Rica? Why or why not?

Internet Activity

Go to the Internet to find out interesting facts about your town, city, or country. What is the current population? Find a picture of your town or city and talk about it with your class.

Health

CHAPTER FIVE

Sleep

Pre-Reading Activity

Discuss these questions.

1. How much sleep do we need?
2. Do many people have problems falling asleep?
3. What do you do when you can't sleep?

Key Vocabulary

Do you know these words? Match the words with the meanings.

1. ＿＿ an average
2. ＿＿ to fall asleep
3. ＿＿ an adult
4. ＿＿ let's say
5. ＿＿ a statesman
6. ＿＿ an inventor

a. to begin to sleep
b. a person who is not a child
c. a person who is first to get an idea for something
d. what you get when you add three numbers and divide the total by three
e. suppose; imagine
f. a man who is a leader in politics

Sleep is very important. Did you know that sleep is more important than food? A person who does not sleep dies faster than a person who does not eat.

Let's say you go to sleep 12 hours late. It will take your body about three weeks to return to normal. We spend about a third (1/3) of our lives in sleep. That's about 121 days a year!

How much sleep do we need? We are all different. A baby needs 16 hours of sleep every day. Children 6 to 12 years old need **an average** of 10 to 12 hours of sleep. Teenagers need 9 to 10 hours of sleep. **An adult** needs an average of 7 to 8 hours a night. There are some people who need only 3 hours of sleep. Others need 10 hours of sleep. After the age of 50, the average sleep time goes down to 6.5 hours a night. We need less sleep as we get older.

Most people have some nights when they cannot sleep. About one in three Americans has a problem with sleep. Many of these people cannot **fall asleep.** The name of this problem is insomnia. The word *insomnia* means "no sleep." Some people say, "I didn't sleep all night." But that's not really true. They may sleep lightly and wake up several times. In the morning, they only remember the times they were awake, so they think they were awake all night.

This is not a new problem. Many famous people in history had insomnia. Some of these people had special ideas to make them sleep. Benjamin Franklin, the famous **statesman** and **inventor,** had four beds. He moved from one to the other to fall asleep. King Louis XIV of France had 413 beds and hoped to fall asleep in one of them. Mark Twain, the famous American writer, had a different way. He lay on his side across the end of the bed!

Vocabulary

Meaning

Complete the sentences. Circle the letter of the correct answer.

1. After the age of 50, people sleep ——————— of 6.5 hours a night.
   a. an average
   b. a third

2. ——————— you don't sleep one day.
   a. Let's talk
   b. Let's say

3. Some people cannot ———————. They call this problem insomnia.
   a. get asleep
   b. fall asleep

4. ——————— needs an average of 7 to 8 hours of sleep every day.
   a. A teenager
   b. An adult

5. Benjamin Franklin was ———————.
   a. an inventor
   b. a sportsman

6. Benjamin Franklin was also ———————.
   a. a French king
   b. a statesman

Vocabulary Activity

Choose the correct answer. Then use the answer in a complete sentence.

1. Which of the following is a good thing to do to fall asleep?

    going shopping   reading a difficult book   cooking

    Example: _Reading a difficult book is a good thing to do to fall asleep._

2. Which of the following is or was a statesman?

    George Bush   Picasso   Mohammed Ali

3. Which of the following was an inventor?

    Gandhi   Thomas Edison   Shakespeare

4. What is the average of 11, 16, and 18?

    16   15   45

5. At what age are you an adult?

    14   21   12

Comprehension

Looking for the Main Ideas

Circle the letter of the best answer.

1. The number of hours we sleep _____.
   a. is the same for all adults
   b. is different for everybody
   c. gets higher as we get older

2. People who have a problem with sleep_____.
   a. are Americans
   b. are famous
   c. have insomnia

3. Benjamin Franklin, King Louis XIV of France, and Mark Twain all had _____.
   a. insomnia
   b. four beds
   c. no ideas

Looking for Details

Circle T if the sentence is true. Circle F if the sentence is false.

1. Some people need only 3 hours of sleep a night.   T   F

2. After age 50, the average sleep time is 6.5 hours a night.   T   F

3. One in four Americans has a problem with sleep.   T   F

4. We spend about a quarter of our lives in sleep.   T   F

5. Benjamin Franklin had four beds.   T   F

6. Mark Twain was a famous statesman.   T   F

Discussion

Find out from the students in your class how they sleep. Fill out the chart below.

Name	Number of Hours of Sleep Each Night	Do You Get Up in the Night?	Do You Dream?
Klara	9	sometimes	no

Discuss these questions with your classmates.

1. What kinds of things do people eat or drink to help them sleep?
2. What kinds of things make you sleep badly or lose sleep?
3. What things do you need in a room to be able to sleep?

Use **when** to show that two things happen at the same time. Notice the use of the comma when the sentence starts with **when.**

Examples:

I have the lights on **when** I sleep.
When I sleep, I have the lights on.

Extra Vocabulary

to snore = to make noise when you sleep
to dream = to see pictures in your sleep
a nightmare = a bad dream

Exercise 1

Join the two sentences with **when.** Begin your sentence with **when.** Use the correct punctuation.

1. I sleep. I have the radio on.

   _____

   _____

2. I sleep. I snore.

   _____

   _____

3. I sleep. I move about a lot.

   _____

   _____

4. I sleep. I like to hold something.

_____

_____

5. I sleep. I lie on my side.

_____

_____

6. I have problems. I cannot sleep.

_____

_____

7. I eat too much. I have a nightmare.

_____

_____

8. I am in a different bed. I cannot sleep.

_____

_____

Exercise 2

Find the mistakes. There are 10 mistakes in grammar and punctuation. Find and correct them.

Sleep very important is. It is most important than food. When a person does not eat he or she dies. When a person does not sleep he or she dies more fast. Baby need the more sleep. Teenager sleep more long than adults. People need less sleep as they get oldest.

Writing Practice

1. Write sentences.

    Answer these questions with complete sentences.

    a. How much sleep do you need?

    _____

    _____

    b. What time do you usually go to bed, and what time do you get up
        in the morning?

    _____

    _____

    c. Are the lights in your room on or off when you sleep? Is the window
        open or closed? Is your room quiet, or is there noise?

    _____

    _____

    d. How often do you wake up in the middle of the night—every day or
        sometimes? What do you do when you wake up?

    _____

    _____

    e. How do you usually sleep—on your back, side, or stomach? Do you
        move about a lot?

    _____

    _____

2. Rewrite in paragraph form.

   Rewrite your sentences in the form of a paragraph. Then check the checklist.

   ### Checklist

   ____ Did you indent the first line?
   ____ Did you give your paragraph a title?
   ____ Did you write the title with a capital letter?
   ____ Did you put the title in the center at the top of the page?
   ____ Did you write on every other line?

3. Edit your work.

   Work with a partner or your teacher to edit your sentences. Correct spelling, punctuation, vocabulary, and grammar.

4. Write your final copy.

CHAPTER SIX

Laughter

Pre-Reading Activity

Discuss these questions.

1. Describe the people in the picture.
2. Who are some well-known funny people in your country?
3. How do you feel after you laugh?

Key Vocabulary

Do you know these words? Match the words with the meanings.

1. _____ muscles
2. _____ an organ
3. _____ blood pressure
4. _____ heartbeat
5. _____ brain
6. _____ a painkiller
7. _____ relaxation
8. _____ circulation

a. measurement of the force of blood moving around the body

b. something that is not work; something that you enjoy

c. a medicine that stops pain

d. movement of the blood around the body

e. the action of the heart

f. what is on your bones that helps you move

g. a part of the body that has a special job (for example, the heart)

h. the organ in the head used for thinking

Laughter

Some people say that laughter is the best medicine. Scientists are beginning to agree with this. They are studying laughter seriously and are finding that it is really good for us.

So what happens when we laugh? We use fifteen different **muscles** in our face, and laughing is good for every **organ** in our body. When we laugh, we breathe quickly and exercise the face, shoulders, and chest. Our **blood pressure** goes down, and our **circulation** gets better. Our **heartbeat** is lower, and our **brain** makes a natural **painkiller** called a beta-endorphin.

Every minute we laugh is the same as forty-five minutes of **relaxation.** Many doctors around the world believe that laughter helps us get better when we are sick.

Today, there are laughter clubs around the world. They try to improve people's health with laughter. The laughter clubs started in India. Now they are all around the world. There are more than 450 laughter clubs just in India. All kinds of people join a laughter club. They go once a day for 20 minutes and start to laugh. There are no jokes. People laugh as a kind of exercise, and everyone feels better afterwards. Some people pay a lot of money to join a laughter club and just laugh.

Of course, there are many kinds of laughter. We may change the way we laugh in different situations. But we all have a laugh that is special to us. How do you usually laugh?

Here's a joke to make you laugh:

Doctor! Doctor! Every time I drink coffee, I get a sharp pain in my eye.

Doctor: Well, take out the spoon.

Vocabulary

Meaning

Complete the sentences. Circle the letter of the correct answer.

1. When we laugh, we use fifteen different _____ in our face.
   a. painkillers
   b. muscles

2. Laughter is good for every _____ in our body.
   a. organ
   b. face

3. When we laugh, our _____ goes down.
   a. blood pressure
   b. brain

4. Laughter makes our _____ better.
   a. medicine
   b. circulation

5. A beta-endorphin is _____.
   a. an exercise
   b. a natural painkiller

6. Laughter makes our _____ lower.
   a. chest
   b. heartbeat

7. Laughter makes a natural painkiller in our _____.
   a. shoulders
   b. brain

8. Forty-five minutes of _____ is the same as one minute of laughter.
   a. relaxation
   b. circulation

Vocabulary Activity

Choose the correct answer. Then use the answer in a complete sentence.

1. Which of the following is relaxation for most people?

   watching television   studying   driving in traffic

2. Which of the following is an organ in the body?

   a leg   a hand   the brain

3. Muscles can be found in which of the following?

   our nails   our legs   our hair

4. Which of these activities makes your heartbeat faster?

   sleeping   running   eating

5. What do you need a painkiller for?

   a joke   a bath   a headache

Comprehension

Looking for the Main Ideas

Circle the letter of the best answer.

1. Scientists say that laughter _____.
   a. is good for us
   b. is serious
   c. is not really good

2. Laughter is good for _____.
   a. our body
   b. only the face
   c. only the chest and shoulders

3. Laughter clubs _____.
   a. are only in India
   b. are places to learn jokes
   c. help people feel better

Looking for Details

One word in each sentence is not correct. Rewrite the sentence with the correct word.

1. We use fifty different muscles in our face.

   _____

   _____

2. Laughing is good for every organ in our brain.

   _____

   _____

3. Every minute we laugh is the same as forty-five hours of relaxation.

   _____

   _____

4. We may change the way we laugh in different shoulders.

   _____

   _____

5. When we laugh, we breathe seriously.

   _____

   _____

6. Our face makes a natural painkiller.

   _____

   _____

Discussion

Find out how the students in your class laugh.
1. How many students laugh with their mouths open?
2. How many students laugh loudly?
3. How many students have a shy and quiet laugh?
4. How many students never laugh?

Adverbs

An *adverb* tells you something about a verb. It answers the question "How?" It usually comes after the verb.

Example:

When we laugh, we <u>breathe</u> <u>quickly.</u>
                             (Verb)   (Adverb)

We usually form an adverb by adding **-ly** to an adjective.

Example:

Adjective	**Adverb**
loud	loudly
quiet	quietly

Exercise 1

Change the adjectives in parentheses into adverbs and rewrite the sentences.

1. She laughs (free).

   _____

   _____

2. He laughs (loud).

   _____

   _____

3. She laughs (shy).

   _____

   _____

4. He laughs (nervous).

   _____

   _____

5. They are studying (serious).

   _____

   _____

6. He speaks (quiet).

   _____

   _____

Exercise 2

Write five sentences about yourself, using these adverbs:

quickly	quietly	seriously
slowly	loudly	

1. _____

   _____

2. _____

   _____

3. _____

   _____

4. _____

   _____

5. _____

   _____

Find the mistakes. There are 10 mistakes in grammar, punctuation, and capitalization. Find and correct them.

Scientist are studying laughter serious. They are finding that laughter is goodly for us. When people are sick laughter helps them to get more better. Laughter club started in india. People join a laughter club and go very day. They may laugh loud for minutes and feel best afterwards.

Extra Vocabulary

> **a joke** = something that you say or do that makes people laugh
>
> **to be embarrassed** = to feel uncomfortable because of something you did or did not do

Writing Practice

1. Write sentences.

   Answer these questions with complete sentences.

   a. Choose one of the following sentences and copy it below.
       I like to laugh a lot.
       I don't like to laugh.
       I sometimes laugh.

       _____

       _____

   b. What things make you laugh (jokes, funny situations, being
       embarrassed)?

       _____

       _____

   c. When did you laugh last?

       _____

       _____

   d. What happened? Who was with you? Where were you?

       _____

       _____

   e. Did you laugh quietly or loudly?

       _____

       _____

   f. Do you feel like laughing when you think of this situation?

       _____

       _____

2. Rewrite in paragraph form.

> Rewrite your sentences in the form of a paragraph. Then check the checklist.

> ### Checklist

> _____ Did you indent the first line?
> _____ Did you give your paragraph a title?
> _____ Did you write the title with a capital letter?
> _____ Did you put the title in the center at the top of the page?
> _____ Did you write on every other line?

3. Edit your work.

> Work with a partner or your teacher to edit your sentences. Correct spelling, punctuation, vocabulary, and grammar.

4. Write your final copy.

Do you know these interesting facts about your body?

Circle T if the sentence is true. Circle F if the sentence is false.

1. You use seventy-two muscles to say one word.   T   F
2. It takes five seconds for blood to go all around your body.   T   F
3. The color of your blood inside your body is blue.   T   F
4. You can't sneeze with your eyes open.   T   F
5. When you start to cry, you feel worse.   T   F
6. Your hair grows faster at night.   T   F

Video Activity • Remedies for Insomnia   CNN

1. What kinds of things do you think can cause insomnia? What kind of remedies do you think can help cure insomnia?

2. Read the following sentences and decide if they are true or false. Then watch the video and check your answers.

   a. One in ten Americans has insomnia.   T   F
   b. Insomnia can cause poor memory.   T   F
   c. Tired drivers cause 10,000 car accidents a year.   T   F
   d. Stress is a common cause of insomnia.   T   F
   e. Writing down your problems can help you sleep better. T   F

3. Which advice on the video do you think is the best? What other advice would you add?

Internet Activity

Go to the Internet to find a good web site for jokes and humor. Tell your class about it.

Customs

CHAPTER SEVEN

Choosing a Name for a Baby

Hindu children are often named after Hindu gods.

Pre-Reading Activity

Discuss these questions.

1. What do you see in the pictures?
2. What special ceremonies or celebrations does your family have for a baby?
3. In your country, who gives the baby a name and when?

Key Vocabulary

Do you know these words? Match the words with the meanings.

1. ___ a ceremony
2. ___ a priest
3. ___ tongue
4. ___ a planet
5. ___ honey
6. ___ a horoscope
7. ___ to suggest
8. ___ to bless

a. a representative of a religion
b. a special event (like a wedding) with special customs
c. sweet liquid made by bees
d. statements about a person's future, made by looking at the stars and planets
e. the organ in your mouth that you speak and taste with
f. a body (like the earth) that moves around a star (like the sun) in space
g. to ask God to make something pure
h. to recommend or advise

Choosing a Name for a Baby

About one billion people live in India. Most of these people are Hindu. The Hindu religion is also a way of life. In the Hindu religion, there are special **ceremonies** for important times in a person's life. There are sixteen ceremonies in all. For each ceremony there is a special fire, and **priests** say prayers and read from a special book. One of these ceremonies is choosing a name for a baby.

The birth of a baby is a happy time in a Hindu family. Soon after the baby is born, the parents wash the baby and write the word *om* on the baby's **tongue.** They write the word in **honey** with a pen of gold. *Om* is a special word in the Hindu religion. Hindus say this word over and over again when they are praying.

Twelve days after the baby is born, a priest visits the family to name the baby. The priest makes **a horoscope** for the baby. To make this horoscope, the priest writes down where the stars and **planets** were at the time the baby was born. From this, he reads the baby's future and **suggests** a good name for the baby. Many children have names of Hindu gods and goddesses or have names with other religious meanings.

At the ceremony, there are guests. The mother holds the baby. The father is on one side. In front of them, there is a plate with rice on it. The father uses a long, thin piece of gold to write the name of the family god, the baby's name, and the date of birth in the rice. Then he says the baby's name in the baby's right ear. The priest then **blesses** the baby. He also blesses the candies and food and then passes them to the guests. This ends the ceremony of giving a name to a baby.

Vocabulary

Meaning

Complete the sentences with the words below.

horoscope   tongue
priest   honey
blesses   ceremony
planets   suggests

1. The Hindus have a _____ to give a name to a baby.

2. The parents write the special word on the baby's _____.

3. They write the word in _____ because most babies like sweet things.

4. A religious man or _____ visits the family twelve days after the baby is born.

5. The priest looks at the positions of the _____ and stars in the sky.

6. He makes a _____ for the new baby from the position of the stars and planets.

7. The priest says what he thinks is a good name. He _____ a name for the baby.

8. At the end of the ceremony, the priest _____ the baby and the food.

Vocabulary Activity

Answer the questions. Use complete sentences.

1. What color clothes does a priest in your religion wear?

   Example: In Buddhism, priests wear bright colors.

   _____

   _____

2. What is an important ceremony in a person's life?

   _____

   _____

3. What is your sign (for your horoscope)?

   _____

   _____

4. What is the name of a planet?

   _____

   _____

5. How do you use honey?

   _____

   _____

6. What can burn or hurt your tongue?

   _____

   _____

Comprehension

Looking for the Main Ideas

Write complete answers to these questions.

1. What religion has sixteen special ceremonies for important times in a person's life?

   _____

   _____

2. What do Hindu people do after a baby is born?

   _____

   _____

3. Why does the priest visit the family?

   _____

   _____

Looking for Details

Circle T if the sentence is true. Circle F if the sentence is false.

1. About a million people live in India.   T   F

2. Most Indians are Hindu.   T   F

3. There are sixteen important ceremonies for each Hindu.   T   F

4. Hindu parents write the word *om* in gold on the tongue
   of their new baby.   T   F

5. At the naming ceremony, there is a plate with rice on it.   T   F

6. The father says the baby's name in the priest's right ear.   T   F

Discussion

Discuss these questions with your classmates.

1. Do you believe in horoscopes? Why or why not?
2. What is the meaning of your name?
3. Do you like your name? Would you change it?

Count Nouns and Noncount Nouns

Count nouns name things that can be counted. *Noncount nouns* name things that cannot be counted.

When a noun is a count noun:

1. You can put *a* or *an* in front of it.

    Example:
    There is **a** guest.

2. It has a plural form.

    Example:
    There are **guests.**

3. You can put a number in front of it.

    Example:
    one guest, **two** guests

When a noun is a noncount noun:

1. You cannot put *a* or *an* in front of it.

    Example:
    There is milk.

2. It usually does not have a plural form.

    Example:
    There is lots of milk.

3. You cannot put a number in front of it.

Note: You can use *lots of* or *a lot of* before both a count noun and a noncount noun.

There are many noncount nouns in English. Here are some of them. You may add other noncount nouns to the list.

Materials/Food	Abstract Nouns	Activities/Subjects	General Nouns
food	luck	dancing	money
fruit	happiness	music	jewelry
gold	love	singing	clothing
hair	fun	homework	furniture
corn	intelligence	grammar	mail
salt	advice	work	cash

Note: Food, fruit, and *hair* can also be count nouns.

Now underline all the nouncount nouns in the reading.

Exercise 1

Look at the underlined noun in each sentence. Circle C if it is a count noun. Circle NC if it is a noncount noun.

1. Hindu is a <u>religion.</u>   C   NC

2. There is a special <u>fire.</u>   C   NC

3. They write the word *om* on the baby's <u>tongue.</u>   C   NC

4. They write the word in <u>honey.</u>   C   NC

5. The priest visits the <u>family.</u>   C   NC

6. He looks at the <u>stars.</u>   C   NC

7. He makes a <u>horoscope.</u>   C   NC

8. He suggests a <u>name.</u>   C   NC

9. There is a <u>plate.</u>   C   NC

10. The plate has <u>rice</u> on it.   C   NC

11. He uses a piece of <u>gold.</u>   C   NC

12. The priest blesses the <u>food.</u>   C   NC

Exercise 2

Write *a, an,* or *some* in front of each word.

1. We have _____ gift.

2. They have _____ food.

3. She has _____ dollar.

4. He has _____ animal.

5. We see _____ people.

6. They give _____ gold.

7. I listen to _____ music.

8. I have _____ idea.

Make sentences using the following words.

1. food

   Example: <u>We have a lot of food at the party.</u>

   _____

   _____

2. money

   _____

   _____

3. music

   _____

   _____

4. dancing

   _____

   _____

Exercise 4

Find the mistakes. There are 10 mistakes in grammar and capitalization. Find and correct them.

There are about one billions people in india. Most of the people are of the hindu religion. This is the most large religion in asia. It is also the world's older religion. A person cannot become a hindu. You are born hindu or you are not. There are also muslims, christians, and other religions, too.

Writing Practice

1. Write sentences.

    Answer these questions with complete sentences.

    a. What is the name of a special day in your country (for example,
        name day, sixteenth birthday)?

        _____

        _____

    b. On what day or days do people celebrate it?

        _____

        _____

    c. Is it a religious day or some other kind of day?

        _____

        _____

    d. What do people do on this day?
        • Do people wear special clothes?
        • Do they have a party at home, or do they go out?
        • Do they cook a lot of food?
        • Is there music or dancing?
        • Do people bring gifts? If so, what kind?

        _____

        _____

    e. Why is this day important?

        _____

        _____

2. Rewrite in paragraph form.

>   Rewrite your sentences in the form of a paragraph. Then check the checklist.

>   **Checklist**
>   ____ Did you indent the first line?
>   ____ Did you give your paragraph a title?
>   ____ Did you write the title with a capital letter?
>   ____ Did you put the title in the center at the top of the page?
>   ____ Did you write on every other line?

3. Edit your work.

>   Work with a partner or your teacher to edit your sentences. Correct spelling, punctuation, vocabulary, and grammar.

4. Write your final copy.

CHAPTER EIGHT

Table Customs in Thailand

Pre-Reading Activity

Discuss these questions.

1. Describe how the person in the picture is eating.

2. In what countries do people not use knives for eating? What do they use?

3. Where does a guest or an important person usually sit at the table in your country?

Key Vocabulary

Do you know these words? Match the words with the meanings.

1.	____ chopsticks	a.	a person who receives guests
2.	____ a bowl	b.	two thin sticks of wood used to eat food
3.	____ to offer	c.	to fill again
4.	____ a host	d.	a deep, round dish, like a dish used for soup
5.	____ to insist	e.	to say politely that you are ready to do or give
6.	____ to refill		something
7.	____ to keep an eye on	f.	to watch over
		g.	to say something strongly

Table Customs in Thailand

Table customs are different around the world. If you are in Thailand, this information will help you.

In Thailand, people do not eat with **chopsticks,** like in China, Japan, and Korea. They use spoons and forks. They never use knives. Most food is already cut. If you need to cut things, use the side of your spoon first and then use your fork. The spoon is more important than the fork. If you are right-handed, keep the spoon in your right hand and the fork in your left hand.

People usually have rice in a separate **bowl.** The rice is not on the same plate with the other food. It is not necessary to finish all your rice or all your food. It is good to leave a little on your plate. If you eat everything, it means you want more.

People always **offer** you more food. The **host** will ask you two or three times if you want more food. First, you must say no. Then the host **insists** again, and you must say no again. The host insists a third time, and you finally say yes and take a little. If you really don't want any more, take very little and leave it on your plate. It is the same with whatever you are drinking. During the meal, never empty your cup or glass. When it is less than half full, your host or neighbor will **refill** it. Never fill your own glass. Always refill your neighbor's glass. This means that you must **keep an eye on** your neighbor's glass all through the meal.

The most important place at a table is at the middle. An important guest will sit at the middle of the table on one side, and the host will sit at the middle of the table on the other side. This may be confusing when the table is round, but the Thai get it right somehow.

Vocabulary

Meaning

Complete the sentences with the words below.

insist	offer
chopsticks	host
bowl	keep an eye on
refill	

1. Chinese people eat their food with —————. The Thai use a spoon and fork.

2. The Thai eat rice in a separate —————.

3. At a dinner, the ————— will seat a guest at the table.

4. The host will ————— you more food.

5. The host will ————— two or three times.

6. You must not ————— your glass or cup. The host or your neighbor will do this.

7. At the table, you must ————— your neighbor's glass and fill it when it is half full.

Vocabulary Activity

Answer the questions. Use complete sentences.

1. What do you keep an eye on in class?

   Example: I keep an eye on the clock in class.

   _____

   _____

2. What do you eat in a bowl?

   _____

   _____

3. What do you offer a visitor to your house?

   _____

   _____

4. In what country do people use chopsticks to eat food?

   _____

   _____

5. When a guest comes to your house, who is usually the host?

   _____

   _____

6. When you eat out, what can you refill?

   _____

   _____

Comprehension

Looking for the Main Ideas

Write complete answers to these questions.

1. What do people in Thailand eat with?

   _____

   _____

2. How many times does the host ask if you want more food?

   _____

   _____

3. What is the most important place for a guest at a table?

   _____

   _____

Looking for Details

Circle T if the sentence is true. Circle F if the sentence is false.

1. The Thai generally do not use knives when they eat.   T   F

2. If you are right-handed, you must keep your fork in
   your right hand.   T   F

3. You must always empty your cup or glass.   T   F

4. You do not fill your own glass.   T   F

5. If you need to cut food, you use your fork.   T   F

6. If you do not want more food, you must leave some
   food on your plate.   T   F

Discussion

Discuss these questions with your classmates.
1. How are table customs in Thailand different from those in your country?
2. How are table customs in the United States different from those in your country?
3. How many kinds of dishes do you usually have at dinner in your country?
4. What is not polite at the table in your country?

Prepositional Phrases

A *phrase* is a group of words. A *prepositional phrase* begins with a preposition. The preposition always has an object. The *object of a preposition* can be a noun or a pronoun.

Examples:

The Thai do not eat   with   chopsticks.
                 (Preposition)   (Object of preposition)

Keep the spoon   in   your right hand.
            (Preposition)   (Object of preposition)

Sometimes there is more than one prepositional phrase in a sentence.

Example:

The rice is not   on the same plate   with your food.
           (Prepositional phrase)   (Prepositional phrase)

Sometimes a prepositional phrase comes at the beginning of a sentence.

Example:

During the meal, drink so that your cup is never empty.
   (Prepositional phrase)

The following are some common prepositions:

about	at	down	of	to
above	before	during	on	under
across	behind	for	out	until
after	below	from	over	up
against	beside	in	since	with
among	between	into	through	without
around	by	near	till	

Underline the prepositional phrase (PP) in these sentences.

1. Use the side of your spoon.

   Example: Use the side <u>of your spoon.</u>

PP

2. Table customs are different around the world.

3. Keep the fork in your left hand.

4. People usually serve rice in a separate bowl.

5. The most important place at a table is at the middle.

6. It is good to leave a little food on your plate.

Complete the sentences with the correct preposition.

1. The Thai usually have dinner _____ six in the evening.

2. We eat _____ a knife and fork.

3. We put soup _____ a bowl.

4. We usually drink tea _____ the end of the meal.

5. We have dinner _____ the dining room.

6. In my country, it is not polite to eat _____ fingers.

Find the mistakes. There are 10 mistakes in grammar and punctuation. Find and correct them.

Thai food is deliciously. They eat a lot of vegetable, seafood, rices, and noodle. When you eat Thai food it is usually spicy. They usually have breakfast from 7:30 to 9 at the morning. They have tea and rices. They drink tea without sugars, milks, or lemon. The Thai do not eat cheeses.

Writing Practice

1. Write sentences.

   Answer these questions with complete sentences.

   a. What time do people in your country usually have dinner?

   _____

   _____

   b. What is on the table (bowls, glasses, cups, different kinds of food, bread, rice)?

   _____

   _____

   c. What does each person have (a bowl, a plate, a napkin)?

   _____

   _____

   d. What do you eat with?

   _____

   _____

   e. What do you eat?

   _____

   _____

   f. What is not polite at the table in your country?

   _____

   _____

2. Rewrite in paragraph form.

> Rewrite your sentences in the form of a paragraph. Then check the checklist.

Checklist

____ Did you indent the first line?
____ Did you give your paragraph a title?
____ Did you write the title with a capital letter?
____ Did you put the title in the center at the top of the page?
____ Did you write on every other line?

3. Edit your work.

> Work with a partner or your teacher to edit your sentences. Correct spelling, punctuation, vocabulary, and grammar.

4. Write your final copy.

Do you know these interesting facts about customs?

Circle T if the answer is true. Circle F if the answer is false.

1. The ancient Romans used to break a cake over the head of a bride to bring happiness.   T   F

2. In Fiji, to show respect to someone, you fold your arms in front of you.   T   F

3. In Sweden, it is the custom to eat with a fork in the right hand.   T   F

4. In Iceland, the names in a telephone book are first names instead of last names.   T   F

5. In Scotland, it is OK to eat on the street.   T   F

6. It is a custom in France for the man to offer his hand first when a man and a woman meet.   T   F

7. When an Inuit tells friends a funny story, the Inuit turns his or her back and faces the wall.   T   F

Video Activity • Changing Customs in China   CNN

1. What are traditional wedding clothes in your country? Describe the clothes that the bride and groom wear.

2. Having a special photo of your wedding day is a custom in many countries. In China, this custom is changing. Watch the video and find out how it is changing. Then make notes about traditional and Western styles of wedding photos in China.

Traditional	Western
brightly colored clothing	

3. Do you think it is good for traditional customs to change? Why? Why not?

Internet Activity

What does your name mean? Go to the Internet to find a web site that tells you the meaning of your name.

Food

CHAPTER NINE

Chocolate

Pre-Reading Activity

Discuss these questions.

1. How often do you eat chocolate?
2. What kinds of foods can have chocolate in them?
3. Do you think chocolate is good for you?

Key Vocabulary

Do you know these words? Match the words with the meanings.

1. ＿＿ hot
2. ＿＿ bitter
3. ＿＿ to add
4. ＿＿ instead of
5. ＿＿ a chocolate bar
6. ＿＿ energy
7. ＿＿ a chemical

a. in place of
b. making your mouth burn from the pepper
c. having a strong taste, like coffee with no sugar
d. a piece of chocolate in the shape of a rectangle
e. the power to be active and work and play
f. something that works by chemistry to have a special effect, often on the body
g. to put together with something else

Chocolate

The Aztecs of Mexico knew about chocolate a long time ago. They made it into a drink. Sometimes they put **hot** chili peppers with the chocolate. They called the drink *xocoatl,* which means "**bitter** juice." This is where the word *chocolate* comes from.

The Spanish went to Mexico and took the drink from the land of the Aztecs back to Spain. The Spanish didn't like peppers, so they **added** sugar. They also liked to drink chocolate hot, and hot chocolate was born. This drink became very popular in Europe. People added different things like eggs to the chocolate drink. But everybody's favorite was chocolate in milk **instead of** water.

There was still no hard chocolate until around 1850. Then the British made the first **chocolate bar.** Twenty-five years later, two men in Switzerland mixed milk with the hard chocolate. Milk chocolate soon became a favorite all over the world.

Is chocolate good for you? For hundreds of years, people thought that chocolate was good for health. Doctors told people to have a chocolate drink for headaches and many other problems. Today, there is good news for chocolate lovers. Scientists think that a little bit of chocolate is good for you! It gives you **energy** and has vitamins to keep your body healthy.

The Aztecs believed that chocolate made you intelligent. Today, we do not believe this. But chocolate has a special **chemical** called phenylethylamine. This is the same chemical the body makes when a person is in love. Which do you prefer—eating chocolate or being in love?

Vocabulary

Meaning

Circle the letter of the correct answer.

1. The Aztecs liked —————— food like chili peppers.
   a. hot
   b. hard

2. The Aztecs drank —————— chocolate.
   a. bitter
   b. sweet

3. The Spanish —————— sugar to the chocolate drink.
   a. called
   b. added

4. People liked to use milk —————— water for a chocolate drink.
   a. with
   b. instead of

5. The first hard chocolate was a British ——————.
   a. chocolate bit
   b. chocolate bar

6. Chocolate is good for the body. It gives people ——————.
   a. energy
   b. intelligence

7. Chocolate has phenylethylamine. This is a ——————.
   a. vitamin
   b. chemical

Vocabulary Activity

Answer the questions. Use complete sentences.

1. Let's say you can't eat chocolate. What do you eat instead of chocolate?

   Example: Instead of chocolate, I eat fruit.

   _____

   _____

2. What is the name of your favorite chocolate bar?

   _____

   _____

3. What food or drink gives you energy?

   _____

   _____

4. What is something that is bitter?

   _____

   _____

5. What do you add to food to make it sweet?

   _____

   _____

6. What do you add to food to make it hot?

   _____

   _____

Comprehension

Looking for the Main Ideas

Circle the letter of the best answer.

1. The Aztecs made _____.
   a. chili peppers into a drink
   b. chocolate into a drink
   c. chocolate peppers

2. The Spanish _____.
   a. were the first to know about chocolate
   b. gave chocolate to the Aztecs
   c. took the chocolate drink to Europe

3. Chocolate _____.
   a. has a special chemical
   b. has no special chemicals
   c. makes you love chemicals

Looking for Details

Circle T if the sentence is true. Circle F if the sentence is false.

1.	The Aztecs put sugar into chocolate.	T	F
2.	The word *chocolate* means "bitter juice."	T	F
3.	The Spanish took peppers to Europe.	T	F
4.	In 1850, people began to eat chocolate.	T	F
5.	Switzerland made the first milk chocolate.	T	F
6.	Chocolate has vitamins.	T	F

Discussion

Discuss these questions with your classmates.

1. Why do you think people like chocolate?
2. What is the most popular kind of chocolate in your country?
3. The Aztecs drank chocolate with spices like vanilla or chili peppers. What other kinds of things can you mix with chocolate?
4. How would you create a wonderful chocolate dish?

Writing Instructions

When you write instructions, you must use exact words to describe each step. It is also important to give all the steps in the correct order.

Exercise 1

Look at these pictures. Number them in the correct order. Then fill in the blanks with the words listed below the pictures.

_____ for a few minutes.

_____ the tea into the cup.

_____ some tea into the teapot.

1

Fill the kettle with water.

_____ the water.

_____ the teapot with boiling water.

Fill   Put   Pour   Leave   Boil

Now write the complete sentences in the correct order.

1. _____

2. _____

3. _____

4. _____

5. _____

6. _____

Exercise 2

Write six sentences to show how you make coffee or chocolate.

1. _____
   _____

2. _____
   _____

3. _____
   _____

4. _____
   _____

5. _____
   _____

6. _____
   _____

Find the mistakes. There are 10 mistakes in grammar, punctuation, and capitalization. Find and correct them.

Jackie loves chocolates. When she has money she buys a box of belgian chocolates. They are the most expensivest chocolates. She likes chocolates bitter. She doesn't like the swiss chocolates milk. When she is sadly she eats one piece of chocolate. When she is tired she eats one. After she eats a chocolate Jackie is happy.

Writing Practice

1. **Write sentences.**

    Answer these questions with complete sentences.

    1. Which do you like best: ice cream, cookies, cake, or chocolate?

        _____

        _____

    2. Do you eat this food every day? How many times a week or month do you eat it?

        _____

        _____

    3. When do you eat it (when you are very hungry, when you are sad, on a special day)?

        _____

        _____

    4. What do you eat it with (milk, coffee, alone)? Do you eat it after a meal or between meals?

        _____

        _____

    5. How much do you like this food?

        _____

        _____

2. Rewrite in paragraph form.

Rewrite your sentences in the form of a paragraph. Then check the checklist.

Checklist

_____ Did you indent the first line?
_____ Did you give your paragraph a title?
_____ Did you write the title with a capital letter?
_____ Did you put the title in the center at the top of the page?
_____ Did you write on every other line?

3. Edit your work.

Work with a partner or your teacher to edit your sentences. Correct spelling, punctuation, vocabulary, and grammar.

4. Write your final copy.

CHAPTER TEN

Coffee

Coffee shop, circa 1940.

Pre-Reading Activity

Discuss these questions.

1. Why do you like or not like coffee?
2. What kinds of coffee are there?
3. How do you like to drink your coffee?

Key Vocabulary

Do you know these words? Match the words with the meanings.

1. ____ beans
2. ____ to take care of
3. ____ to boil
4. ____ too
5. ____ liquid
6. ____ to discover
7. ____ excited

a. to heat until it begins to bubble
b. to find something that nobody knew about before you
c. anything that runs or flows like water
d. the seeds of a plant
e. having strong feelings or lots of energy
f. to look after
g. also

Coffee

People all over the world drink coffee. It is the world's most popular drink. The French call it *café,* the Germans *kaffee,* the Japanese *koohi,* the Turkish *kahve.* But the people of Sweden drink the most coffee—more than five cups a day. Over half of American adults drink it every day, but not as much as in Sweden. Too much coffee is bad for your health.

We don't know who really **discovered** coffee. There is a popular story about a young man who discovered coffee in Ethiopia, a country in Africa. Around the year 700, there was a young man called Kaldi who **took care of** goats. One day, he watched them while they were eating some plants. Soon after they ate the plants, the goats became very **excited,** and they did not sleep that night. Kaldi tried the plants himself, and he became very excited, **too.** Other people tried the plants. They decided to **boil** the plants and then drink the **liquid.** They too couldn't sleep well at night. This drink became popular and went from Ethiopia to Arabia. By 1200, it was a popular drink in the Arab world. The word *coffee* comes from the Arab word *qahwah.* Coffee then traveled from Arabia to Turkey, Europe, and the rest of the world.

Coffee has been very popular in history. Many famous people loved coffee. The French writer Voltaire needed seventy-two cups every day. In 1735, the German musician Johann Sebastian Bach wrote music about coffee. Another German musician, Beethoven, counted sixty **beans** for each cup of coffee he made. That was strong!

There are coffee houses and coffee bars all over North America today. There are bars with all kinds of coffee. There are different sizes and flavors. There are bars where you can use the Internet while you drink your coffee!

Vocabulary

Meaning

Complete the sentences. Circle the letter of the correct answer.

1. A young man called Kaldi _____ coffee in Ethiopia.
   a. discovered
   b. grew

2. Kaldi _____ goats.
   a. took care of
   b. discovered

3. When the goats ate the coffee plants, the goats became _____.
   a. popular
   b. excited

4. Other people ate the plants, and they became excited _____.
   a. too
   b. much

5. Some people count how many _____ they want in their coffee.
   a. cups
   b. beans

6. People started to _____ the coffee plants in water.
   a. boil
   b. use

7. Then they drank the _____.
   a. liquid
   b. flavors

Vocabulary Activity

Choose the correct answer. Then use the answer in a complete sentence.

1. Which of the following can make a person excited?

    going to sleep   doing homework   watching a movie

    Example: <u>Watching a movie can make a person excited.</u>

2. Which of the following do we usually boil?

    a tomato   a potato   an orange

3. Which of the following discovered America?

    Christopher Columbus   George Washington   Gandhi

4. Which of the following do we usually take care of?

    a teacher   a baby   a country

Comprehension

Looking for the Main Ideas

Circle the letter of the best answer.

1. Coffee is ——————.
   a. popular only in America
   b. the world's most popular drink
   c. bad for your health

2. A story says ——————.
   a. a young man discovered coffee in Ethiopia
   b. people discovered coffee in Arabia
   c. goats discovered coffee in Turkey

3. Coffee ——————.
   a. has not been popular in history
   b. has been popular in history with musicians
   c. has been popular in history

Looking for Details

Circle T if the sentence is true. Circle F if the sentence is false.

1. The people of Sweden drink five cups of coffee a day.   T   F

2. Coffee went from Ethiopia to Turkey.   T   F

3. The word *coffee* comes from a Turkish word.   T   F

4. The Turkish name for coffee is *kahve*.   T   F

5. Coffee was popular in Arabia first, then in Europe.   T   F

6. Voltaire drank sixty cups of coffee every day.   T   F

Discussion

Discuss these questions with your classmates.

1. What is the most popular drink in your country?
2. What is your favorite drink?
3. Which drink do you not like? Why?

The Pronouns
it and *them*

It is a pronoun. A *pronoun* replaces another word so that you do not repeat the same word too many times.

1. Look back to the reading on coffee.
2. Underline the pronoun **it** in the first paragraph.
3. How many times do you see the pronoun **it?**
4. What does the pronoun **it** replace?

Use the pronoun **it** for singular words. Use the pronoun **them** for plural words.

Example:

Kaldi took care of his goats. He watched **them** while they were eating some plants.

Exercise 1

Replace the repeated word with the correct pronoun.

1. Jack loves coffee. He drinks coffee every morning.

   _____

   _____

2. I can't drink coffee at night. Coffee keeps me awake.

   _____

   _____

3. I usually have coffee with milk, but sometimes I have coffee with cream.

   _____

   _____

4. At four every day, my friend eats cookies. She likes to eat cookies with a cup of coffee.

_____

_____

Find the mistakes. There are 10 mistakes in grammar, punctuation, and capitalization. Find and correct them.

Tony always drink hotly coffee. He drinks it with milk but no

sugars. He doesn't like coffee strong like turkish coffee. His Favorite

is brazilian coffee. He drinks four smalls cups every day. He has a

cup for breakfast and cup at eleven. After lunch, he has a cup.

When he gets home from work he has a cup.

Writing Practice

1. Write sentences.

    Answer these questions with complete sentences.

    1. What is your favorite drink (tea, coffee, hot chocolate, milk, soda)?

        _____

        _____

    2. How do you drink it (in a cup, in a glass, in a bowl, with sugar)?

        _____

        _____

    3. When do you drink it (at breakfast, at meal times, between meals)?

        _____

        _____

    4. How many cups do you drink a day?

        _____

        _____

    5. How much do you like this drink? Can you live without it?

        _____

        _____

2. Rewrite in paragraph form.

Rewrite your sentences in the form of a paragraph. Then check the checklist.

Checklist

____ Did you indent the first line?
____ Did you give your paragraph a title?
____ Did you write the title with a capital letter?
____ Did you put the title in the center at the top of the page?
____ Did you write on every other line?

3. Edit your work.

Work with a partner or your teacher to edit your sentences. Correct spelling, punctuation, vocabulary, and grammar.

4. Write your final copy.

Food Quiz

Match the foods in the pictures with their countries of origin.

Germany   United States
Mexico   China
Austria   Ireland

1. ginger ale
_____

2. chewing gum
_____

3. hot dog
_____

4. spaghetti
_____

5. croissant
_____

6. hamburger
_____

Video Activity • A Healthy Recipe

1. Did you know that tomatoes are good for your heart? They contain lycopene, a chemical that may help prevent heart disease. You are going to learn how to make a healthy tomato soup. First read the list of ingredients and decide the order in which you think they will be used in the recipe. Then watch the video to check your answers.

   _____ pepper   _____ garlic

   _____ can of tomatoes   _____ olive oil

   _____ corn   _____ basil

   _____ onion   _____ water

2. Watch the video again. Then try to write the recipe for tomato soup.

Internet Activity

Which countries produce coffee and chocolate? Go to the Internet to find out where these foods are grown.

Inventions

CHAPTER ELEVEN

Money

Man with Yap stone money.

Pre-Reading Activity

Discuss these questions.

1. What color are paper bills in the United States? Are they all the same color?
2. What color are paper bills in your country? Are they all the same size?
3. Is it a good idea to have bills the same size?
4. What names for money do you know? In which countries are these kinds of money used?

Key Vocabulary

Do you know these words? Match the words to the pictures.

paper bills	feathers	stuck
coins	a pole	string

1.	2.	3.
4.	5.	6.

Money

When we think of money, we think of **coins** and **paper bills.** That is what money is today. But in the past, people used many things as money. Some countries used cows, salt, tea, or butter. Other countries used **feathers** or stones.

People on the island of Santa Cruz in the Pacific Ocean used feather money. They made this money from small red feathers. They **stuck** the feathers together to make **a string.** The string could be up to thirty-two feet long. They used this money to pay for a marriage or to buy a boat.

The island of Yap in the Pacific Ocean is a place where people used and still use the heaviest money in the world: Yap stones. These are round white stones with a hole in the middle. The Yap stones do not come from the island. The Yap men have to go to islands 400 miles away to get them. They work the stones to make them round and then make a hole in the middle. They put **a pole** through the hole so that more than one person can carry the stones. Big stones can be twelve feet high—as big as two tall men. They can weigh more than one ton. Small stones are as big as dinner plates. Rich people do not carry the Yap stones. Servants follow the rich people. Each servant carries a stone on a pole over his shoulder. Today people on the island use paper money for everyday shopping. But for other things they still prefer Yap stones.

Money has changed a lot over the years: from feathers to Yap stones to today's plastic money or credit cards. Money has become a very important part of our lives. Just take a look around you and you can see how important it is.

Vocabulary

Meaning

Complete the sentences with the words below.

string   paper bills
pole   feathers
coins   stuck

1. Today we use —————— made of metal for money.

2. We also use ————— for large amounts of money because they are lighter to carry.

3. In some countries, people used ————— from special birds as money.

4. On the island of Santa Cruz, people ————— the feathers together to make one long piece.

5. When they joined the feathers together, the feathers made a long —————.

6. Yap stones have a hole in the middle. Men put a ————— through the hole to carry the stones.

Vocabulary Activity

Answer the questions. Use complete sentences.

1. Where can you see a pole?

   Example: <u>You can see a pole with a flag on it in front of a government building.</u>

   _____

   _____

2. Where do you put your coins?

   _____

   _____

3. How many paper bills do you have with you today?

   _____

   _____

4. What do you usually stick on an envelope?

   _____

   _____

5. What animal has feathers?

   _____

   _____

6. What do you tie with a string?

   _____

   _____

Comprehension

Looking for the Main Ideas

Circle the letter of the best answer.

1. People —————.
   a. always use paper money and coins
   b. always used coins in the past
   c. still do not use paper money all the time

2. On the island of Santa Cruz, people used ————— as money.
   a. a string
   b. feathers
   c. stones

3. People on the island of Yap sometimes use ————— as money.
   a. stones
   b. two tall men
   c. small stones

Looking for Details

Circle T if the sentence is true. Circle F if the sentence is false.

1. In Santa Cruz, people used feathers to buy a boat.   T   F

2. Yap stones come from the island of Yap.   T   F

3. Yap stones are twelve feet high.   T   F

4. People use small stones for dinner plates.   T   F

5. Servants carry the Yap stones for the rich.   T   F

6. A servant carries a stone on a pole on his shoulder.   T   F

Discussion

Find students in your class who are not from your country. Ask them about money in their country. Then fill out the chart below.

Name	Country	Name of Money	Symbol
Ali	Turkey	lira	TL

Discuss these questions with your classmates.

1. Do you like the idea of using other things, such as tea or stones, as money?

2. Is money the most important thing in life for you?

3. In the United States, people say, "Time is money." Do you agree with this?

4. More and more people are using credit cards. Do you think that one day coins and paper bills will go out of use?

Comparing Things
with *as . . . as*

When you compare two things that are the same, use

as + adjective + as.

Examples:

Big stones can be **as big as** two tall men.
Small stones are **as big as** dinner plates.

For the negative form, use

not as + adjective + as.

Examples:

A dime is **not as big as** a quarter.
Salt is **not as expensive as** tea.

Exercise 1

Make sentences with the words below and a form of the verb *to be*.
When you see the = symbol, use **as . . . as.**
When you see the < symbol, use **not as . . . as.**

1.   A small stone = a dinner plate (big)

   Example: <u>A small stone is as big as a dinner plate.</u>

2.   paper bills < coins (heavy)

   _____

   _____

3.   a cent < a dime (small)

   _____

   _____

4. bicycles < cars (expensive)

    _____

    _____

5. time = money in the United States (important)

    _____

    _____

6. tea = money in some countries (valuable)

    _____

    _____

Exercise 2

Work alone, with a partner, or in a group. Make sentences with the comparative. Use **as . . . as, -er . . . than,** or **more . . . than.**

1. A paper bill in my country / United States dollar bill. (big)

    _____

    _____

2. A car in the United States / a car in my country. (expensive)

    _____

    _____

3. Money / time in my country. (important)

    _____

    _____

Find the mistakes. There are 10 mistakes in grammar and capitalization. Find and correct them.

A long time ago, people used food for moneys. Salt was the popularest money. Then people used thing like stones and feather for money. The first paper money came from china. This was about three thousand year ago. Today we have paper money and coin, but people like to use Credit Card.

Writing Practice

1. Write sentences.

    Answer these questions with complete sentences.

    a. What is the name of the currency (money) in your country?

    _____

    _____

    b. Are the paper bills in your country all one color or different colors?

    _____

    _____

    c. Are the paper bills in your country as big in size as the U.S. dollar bill or bigger?

    _____

    _____

    d. What is the paper bill with the smallest value? What can you buy with it?

    _____

    _____

    e. Are people in your country today using credit cards?

    _____

    _____

    f. Do you think that one day everybody in your country will use credit cards in place of money?

    _____

    _____

2. Rewrite in paragraph form.

Rewrite your sentences in the form of a paragraph. Then check the checklist.

Checklist

____ Did you indent the first line?
____ Did you give your paragraph a title?
____ Did you write the title with a capital letter?
____ Did you put the title in the center at the top of the page?
____ Did you write on every other line?

3. Edit your work.

Work with a partner or your teacher to edit your sentences. Correct spelling, punctuation, vocabulary, and grammar.

4. Write your final copy.

CHAPTER 12

Perfume

Pre-Reading Activity

Discuss these questions.

1. What is your favorite perfume?
2. Why do people use perfume?
3. What is perfume made from?

Key Vocabulary

Do you know these words? Match the words with the meanings.

1. ＿＿ through
2. ＿＿ ancient
3. ＿＿ leather
4. ＿＿ spices
5. ＿＿ drapes
6. ＿＿ an ingredient
7. ＿＿ expert
8. ＿＿ completely

a. very old
b. curtains
c. a person who is very good at a job or knows a lot about a subject
d. one of a mixture of things from which something is made
e. dried plants, like pepper, that give taste to food
f. totally
g. by way of
h. dried animal skin

Perfume

A long time ago, people found a way to create a nice smell. They put nice-smelling wood or leaves into a fire. A nice smell came **through** the smoke. That is how we got the word *perfume.* In Latin, *per* means "through," and *fumus* means "smoke."

In **ancient** times, people used a lot of perfume. The Greeks used different perfumes for different parts of the body. Everybody used perfume, both men and women. When guests came for a special dinner, the host gave them more perfume to put on themselves. The Romans did the same as the Greeks. But they did not just perfume themselves once a day. They perfumed themselves three times a day! They also perfumed their dogs and horses. They perfumed their flags and things around the house such as **drapes** and cushions. Perfume was as important as food.

Today, perfume is not natural as it was in the past. Perfume is also not simple to make. A perfume **expert** must tell the difference among nineteen thousand different smells. Most of these smells are from chemicals; they are not from real flowers. For a very good perfume today, the expert mixes more than a hundred **ingredients.**

Perfume has other uses too. Plastic that smells like **leather** is just one example. Also, scientists are finding that some smells make us feel better. They help us to relax, to sleep, or to feel happier. Scientists found that the smell of apples with **spices** can make our blood pressure go down. In the future, we may use perfume in a **completely** different way.

Perfumes we see in the stores have names of famous designers like Gucci or Chanel on them. Some perfumes even have names of movie stars on them. People buy perfumes not just for the smell, but also for the name.

Vocabulary

Meaning

Complete the sentences with the words below.

drapes	ancient
completely	spices
through	experts
ingredients	leather

1. A long time ago, people put nice-smelling leaves into a fire. Then a nice smell came _____ the smoke.

2. The Greeks in _____ times used a lot of perfume.

3. The Romans perfumed the _____ on their windows too.

4. There are people who can tell the difference among thousands of different smells. They are _____.

5. Today we use perfumes in _____ different ways than people in the past.

6. Sometimes you need more than a hundred _____ to make one perfume.

7. The smell of some _____ we use for food can help us feel better.

8. Today, people can make plastic smell like _____.

Vocabulary Activity

Answer the questions. Use complete sentences.

1. What is something we see through?

   Example: _We see through a window._

   _____

   _____

2. What is something made from leather?

_____

_____

3. What is an ingredient in a cake?

_____

_____

4. What is a spice you like?

_____

_____

5. What is the name of a chemical?

_____

_____

6. What is the name of an ancient place?

_____

_____

Comprehension

Looking for the Main Ideas

Write complete answers to these questions.

1. What does the word *perfume* mean in Latin?

_____

_____

2. Who used a lot of perfume in ancient times?

_____

_____

3. How can smells help you?

_____

_____

Looking for Details

One word in each sentence is not correct. Rewrite the sentence with the correct word.

1. A long time ago, people put nice-smelling plastic or leaves into a fire.

   _____

   _____

2. A perfume expert can tell the difference among ninety thousand different smells.

   _____

   _____

3. Some of the ingredients in perfume today are not from real people.

   _____

   _____

4. Smoke that smells like leather is an example.

   _____

   _____

5. The smell of apples with spices can make our blood pressure go through.

   _____

   _____

Discussion

Discuss these questions with your classmates.

1. What fact about perfume in the reading do you find most interesting or surprising?
2. Some people do not like the smell of other people's perfume in the air around them. Do you think the use of perfume should be stopped?
3. Some smells make people feel better. What smells make you feel better?
4. How do you think perfume will be used in the future?

Using *too* and *very*

Using *too* or *very* + Adjective

Very goes before an adjective. It emphasizes the adjective. It has a positive meaning.

Example:

For a **very** good perfume, an expert uses more than a hundred ingredients.

You must not confuse **very** with **too.** When **too** goes before an adjective, it gives the idea of "more than necessary." **Too** has a negative meaning.

Examples:

That smell is **too** sweet. (I don't like it.)
That smell is **very** sweet. (I like it.)

Exercise 1

Complete the sentences with **too** or **very.**

1. This smell is ———— good. I like it.

2. I don't like this smell. It's ———— strong for me.

3. She likes a strong perfume. This is ———— weak for her.

4. The smell of fresh bread makes me feel ———— hungry.

5. This perfume is ———— expensive. I can never buy it.

6. I love the smell of the rose. It's ———— delicate.

Two Meanings of *too*

Too changes its meaning with the position it has in a sentence. Before an adjective, it has a negative meaning.

Example:

This perfume is **too** strong. (I don't like it.)

At the end of an affirmative sentence, **too** means "also."

Example:

I like that perfume and this one, **too.** (I like it also.)

Note: You should use a comma before **too** when it means "also."

Exercise 2

Rewrite the second sentence in each pair, using **too** in the correct place.

1. I don't like this smell. It is stronger than necessary.

   Example: It is too strong.

2. That perfume has a strong smell. It is also expensive.

   _____

   _____

3. The perfume has real flowers. It also has some chemicals.

   _____

   _____

4. I didn't buy that perfume. It is more expensive than necessary.

   _____

   _____

5. The smell of the sea makes me feel relaxed. It also makes me feel happy.

_____

_____

6. Please don't use that perfume. It is heavier than necessary.

_____

_____

Exercise 3

Find the mistakes. There are 10 mistakes in grammar, capitalization, and punctuation. Find and correct them.

Today we use perfume, but we do not use as much the ancient greeks and romans. They used two much perfume. They perfumed their bodies and their too animals. The Arabs liked too perfume. They roses liked. They made rose water. It is light than rose perfume. It is still popular today.

Writing Practice

1. Write sentences.

   Answer these questions with complete sentences.

   a. What is your favorite perfume or smell?

   _____

   _____

   b. How often do you use it or smell it?

   _____

   _____

   c. Why do you use or not use perfume?

   _____

   _____

   d. Are there any other perfumes or smells that you like?

   _____

   _____

   e. Are there any smells or perfumes that you don't like?

   _____

   _____

   f. Do you think it is important to have nice smells? Why or why not?

   _____

   _____

   g. Do you think people have the right to use perfume when other people may not like it?

   _____

   _____

2. Rewrite in paragraph form.

   Rewrite your sentences in the form of a paragraph. Then check the checklist.

   Checklist
   _____ Did you indent the first line?
   _____ Did you give your paragraph a title?
   _____ Did you write the title with a capital letter?
   _____ Did you put the title in the center at the top of the page?
   _____ Did you write on every other line?

3. Edit your work.

   Work with a partner or your teacher to edit your sentences. Correct spelling, punctuation, vocabulary, and grammar.

4. Write your final copy.

Inventions Quiz

Circle the correct answer.

1. How many countries use a dollar?
    a. ten
    b. twenty-two
    c. forty-seven

2. How long have people had bicycles?
    a. 500 years
    b. 150 years
    c. 50 years

3. Who discovered paper?
    a. the Chinese
    b. the Arabs
    c. the Aztecs

4. When did people first use aspirin tablets?
    a. in 1820
    b. in 1949
    c. in 1915

5. Different countries use different kinds of money. Match the money with the country.

    1. euro   a. Mexico
    2. peso   b. China
    3. yuan   c. Brazil
    4. riyal   d. Germany
    5. cruzeiro   e. Saudi Arabia

Video Activity • Is Your Money Real?

1. Do you have any paper money with you today? Take a look at it. What details of the design make it difficult to copy?

2. You are going to watch a video about the new twenty-dollar bill in the United States. Read the list below. Then watch the video and check which of these design details make it difficult to copy (or counterfeit) this bill.

   ☐ The portrait is bigger.
   ☐ The portrait has more detail.
   ☐ There is a red line.
   ☐ The number 20 has a special design.
   ☐ There are wavy lines behind the portrait.
   ☐ There is a watermark.
   ☐ The number 20 is bigger.
   ☐ The number 20 has three different colors.

3. Do you think it is easier to counterfeit cash or credit cards? Which do you think is safer to carry? Which do you prefer to use and why?

Internet Activity

Choose five countries around the world. Go to the Internet to find the name of the currency each country uses. Then use the information to make a quiz for your classmates.

Example:

What currency do Italians use?

(a) pesos   (b) francs   (c) euros

People

CHAPTER THIRTEEN

Tiger Woods

Pre-Reading Activity

Discuss these questions.

1. Describe the man in the picture.
2. What do you think he is doing?
3. Why do you think he is famous?

Key Vocabulary

Do you know these words? Match the words with the meanings.

1. _____ a homemaker
2. _____ Asian
3. _____ a nickname
4. _____ to save a life
5. _____ amazing
6. _____ a mall
7. _____ a professional
8. _____ to obey

a. a name given to a person by family or friends
b. a person who earns money from an activity, such as playing a sport
c. surprising or shocking in a good way
d. to do what someone asks you to do
e. a person who stays at home to take care of the house and children
f. to stop someone from getting killed
g. from Japan, China, Korea, Indonesia, Thailand, or another country in Asia
h. a building or group of buildings with shops, restaurants, and theaters

Tiger Woods

Tiger Woods was born in California in 1975. His father was in the U.S. Army. His mother is **a homemaker.** She is from Thailand. From his father's side and his mother's side, Tiger is **Asian**, African American, Native American, and European.

Tiger's real name is Eldrick. He got the **nickname** Tiger from his father. His father had a friend in the Vietnam War. The friend's nickname was Tiger. After this friend **saved his life**, Tiger's father decided to give his son the same name.

Tiger's father decided to make his son the best golfer in the world. When Tiger was 6 months old, he watched his father play golf for hours. When he was 2 years old, he started to play golf. For a small child he played very well. Soon he was on TV shows like CBS News. At age 4, Tiger took golf lessons. His teacher said that he was **amazing.** When he was 8, he started to play in a series of games or tournaments. By age 11, he had won thirty championships!

Tiger was a champion at golf, but he was like other children. He watched TV and went to the **mall.** He loved and **obeyed** his parents. They always told him that school was important. Tiger was a good student. He said, "School comes first, golf second."

After high school, Tiger went to Stanford University. During this time, he won many championships. He began to play with the top people in golf. He wanted to be **a professional** like them. Up to then, he did not make money because he was not a professional. So, in 1996, Tiger left college and became a professional. He made millions of dollars. But that did not change him.

In 1997, Tiger played in the most important golf game—the Masters tournament. Tiger won! He was the youngest person to win the tournament. He was also the first African American or Asian American to win the Masters.

Tiger continues to win championships. He is one of the greatest players in the history of golf. He has also changed our ideas about people who play golf.

Vocabulary

Meaning

Complete the sentences with the words below.

Asian	saved
homemaker	nickname
amazing	professional
mall	obeyed

1. Tiger's mother does not work outside the house. She is a _____ .

2. Tiger's mother is from Thailand. She is _____ .

3. Eldrick is his real name. Tiger is his _____ .

4. A man _____ Tiger's father's life in the Vietnam War. His nickname was Tiger.

5. Tiger's teacher could not believe how well Tiger could play golf. Tiger was _____ .

6. Tiger and his friends went to the _____ , where there were stores and restaurants.

7. Tiger was a good son. He always _____ his parents when they told him to do something.

8. Tiger wanted to make money as a golfer, so he became a _____ .

Vocabulary Activity

Answer the questions. Use complete sentences.

1. What is an amazing invention?

    Example: _The computer is an amazing invention._

    _____

    _____

2. What is your or your friend's nickname?

    _____

    _____

3. Who in your family is a homemaker?

    _____

    _____

4. What is a store you find in a mall?

    _____

    _____

5. What is an Asian name or country?

    _____

    _____

6. What people do you usually obey?

    _____

    _____

Comprehension

Looking for the Main Ideas

Circle the letter of the best answer.

1. Tiger is his —————— .
   a. real name
   b. nickname
   c. father's name

2. Tiger's father —————— .
   a. was a golf champion
   b. wanted him to be a great golfer
   c. gave him lessons

3. Tiger was —————— .
   a. the youngest person to win the Masters tournament
   b. not a professional at the time of the Masters tournament
   c. the first American to win the Masters tournament

Looking for Details

One word in each sentence is not correct. Rewrite the sentence with the correct word.

1. When he was 2 years old, Tiger started to watch golf.

   _____

   _____

2. At age 4, Tiger took tennis lessons.

   _____

   _____

3. By age 11, he had won 30 scholarships.

   _____

   _____

4. His parents always told him that golf was important.

_____

_____

5. In 1996, Tiger left home and became a professional.

_____

_____

6. In 1997, Tiger played in the most expensive golf game—the Masters tournament.

_____

_____

Discussion

Discuss these questions with your classmates.

1. Many young people want to be famous sports stars. Would you like to be a famous sports star? Why or why not?
2. Do you like golf? Why or why not?
3. Some professional sports stars make millions of dollars. Do you think this is right?
4. Tiger Woods is a "role model" for young people. He works hard, and he is successful, well-mannered, and a nice person. How important is it for sports stars and movie stars to be role models?

Writing About Time

Asking Questions

Asking the right questions is important when you write about another person's life. In the exercise below, you will write questions to go with the sentences.

Exercise 1

Write the questions for these answers.

1. _____?

    I was born in Tokyo, Japan.

2. _____?

    I was born in 1984.

3. _____?

    My father is an engineer.

4. _____?

    My mother is a homemaker.

5. _____?

    I have two brothers and one sister.

6. _____?

    I went to high school in Tokyo.

7. _____?

    I graduated from high school in 2001.

8. _____?

   Right now, I am studying English.

9. _____?

   In the future, I want to go to an American university.

10. _____?

    I want to study design.

Prepositions of Time

Using *in*

Use **in** with years or months.

Examples:

In 1997, . . .
In December, . . .

Using *from . . . to . . .*

Use **from** for the beginning of an action and **to** for the end of the
action.

Examples:

I went to high school **from** 1996 **to** 2001.
I work **from** nine **to** five.
She was on vacation **from** July 15 **to** August 15.

Using *for*

Use **for** to show how long.

Examples:

I studied English **for** three years.
I stayed in New York **for** ten days.

Write the correct prepositions in the blanks.

1. I arrived in Boston ——————— June for the summer.

2. He lived in Tokyo ——————— sixteen years.

3. She worked for that company ——————— 1995 ——————— 2002.

4. He graduated from high school ——————— 1998.

5. He worked for that company ——————— fifteen years.

6. He worked ——————— six in the morning ——————— eight at night.

7. Tiger Woods was born ——————— 1975.

8. I am going back ——————— December for my vacation.

Exercise 3

Find the mistakes. There are 10 mistakes in grammar, punctuation, and capitalization. Find and correct the mistakes.

Tiger Woods was born to California, but he lives in orlando, florida.

He spends a lot time with his parent. His father, earl, and his

mother, kultida, live too in florida.

Writing Practice

1. **Write sentences.**

   Work with a partner. Find out about your partner's life. Ask questions about the past, the present, and the future.

   These prompts may help you:

   Where / when were you born?
   How many brothers / sisters / have?
   When / go / high school?
   Where / go / high school?
   What / study / now?
   Where / study / now?
   What / do / in the future?
   Why?

   Include any other questions you like. Use the answers to write sentences about your partner.

2. **Rewrite in paragraph form.**

   Rewrite your sentences in the form of a paragraph. Use your partner's name as the title. Then check the checklist.

   Checklist

   ____ Did you indent the first line?
   ____ Did you write the title with a capital letter?
   ____ Did you put the title in the center at the top of the page?
   ____ Did you write on every other line?

3. **Edit your work.**

   Work with a partner or your teacher to edit your sentences. Correct spelling, punctuation, vocabulary, and grammar.

4. **Write your final copy.**

CHAPTER FOURTEEN

Amy Van Dyken

Pre-Reading Activity

Discuss these questions.

1. Describe the woman in the photo.
2. What do you think she is doing?

Key Vocabulary

Do you know these words? Match the words with the meanings.

1. _____ a race
2. _____ a scholarship
3. _____ to train
4. _____ an event
5. _____ a medal
6. _____ to injure
7. _____ sign language
8. _____ deaf (hearing impaired)

a. a round piece of metal, like a big coin, that you get when you win something
b. to hurt a part of the body
c. not able to hear
d. to prepare for an event or test
e. a game or contest to see who can go the fastest
f. one race or game in a group of races or games
g. money given to a student to pay for his or her studies
h. a language spoken with the hands, used to speak with people who cannot hear

Amy Van Dyken

Amy Van Dyken was born in Englewood, Colorado, in 1973. She was a sick child. The doctors told her parents that Amy had asthma. People with asthma sometimes can't breathe. Amy went to the hospital many times when she was young. She couldn't do the things other children could do. Then she started to swim and liked it. When she swam, she could be like all the other children. In the beginning, she was slow. When there was **a race,** she was always the last. It was very hard for her, but she swam faster and faster. When she was 13, she started to win races.

Amy graduated from high school in 1991. She was a good swimmer, so many colleges wanted to give her swimming **scholarships.** She decided to go to the University of Arizona. Two years later, she changed and went to Colorado State University.

In 1994, Amy was College Swimmer of the Year. In the fall of 1994, Amy decided to leave college early. She wanted to **train** for the 1996 Olympics full time. She swam five to six hours a day. During this time, Amy continued her asthma medicine. With all her training, she can still take in only 60% as much air as people without asthma.

When the Olympics arrived in 1996, Amy was ready. She entered five **events.** She did not do well in the first event. But then she won one gold **medal** after another. She won four gold medals! She was the first American woman to win four gold medals in one Olympics.

In 1998, Amy **injured** her shoulder when she was training. She won one race in 1999, but injured her shoulder again. In 2000, Amy entered the Olympics again. She had a bad shoulder, so she did not do as well as in the 1996 Olympics. This time she won two gold medals.

Amy knows **sign language** for the **deaf (hearing impaired)** and plans to work with deaf children. She tells children with asthma to do what they want to do and not to let asthma stop them from doing anything.

Vocabulary

Meaning

Complete the sentences with the words below.

injured	deaf
race	medals
trained	sign language
scholarships	events

1. In the beginning, it was hard for Amy to win a —————.

2. Colleges want good swimmers. Many colleges wanted to give Amy ————— so she could attend college for free.

3. Amy ————— from five to six hours a day to be ready for the Olympics.

4. Amy entered five swimming ————— in the 2000 Olympics.

5. In the 1996 Olympics, Amy got four gold —————.

6. In 1998, Amy had problems because she ————— her shoulder.

7. Amy knows —————, so she can communicate with children who cannot hear.

8. Amy wants to help ————— children. These children cannot hear.

Vocabulary Activity

Choose the correct answer. Then use the answer in a complete sentence.

1. Which of the following do people train for?
   the Olympics   dinner   a walk in the park

   Example: _People train for the Olympics._

2. Who usually gets a scholarship?
   a student   a teacher   a doctor

3. Which of the following can you injure?

 a medal   a knee   a car

4. Which of the following is a race?

 the 100-meter sprint (run)   the ten-minute walk
 the game of tennis

5. Which of the following is an event in the Olympics?

 the 50-meter freestyle   the car race   the 50-meter walk

6. Which of the following is *not* a kind of Olympic medal?

 gold   silver   diamond

Comprehension

Looking for the Main Ideas

Circle the letter of the correct answer.

1. When she was a child, Amy had a problem with _____.
 a. asthma
 b. doctors
 c. other children

2. In 1994, Amy _____.
 a. finished college
 b. left college early
 c. went to the University of Arizona

3. In the Olympic games of 1996, Amy won_____.
 a. because she was a woman
 b. because she was American
 c. four gold medals

Looking for Details

Circle T if the sentence is true. Circle F if the sentence is false.

1. Amy was a strong child.   T   F

2. Many high schools wanted to give Amy scholarships.   T   F

3. After high school, Amy went to Colorado State University.   T   F

4. Amy entered five events in the 1996 Olympics.   T   F

5. Amy injured her shoulder in 1998 and in 1999.   T   F

6. Amy won two gold medals in the 2000 Olympics.   T   F

Discussion

Discuss these questions with your classmates.

1. What personal qualities do you think helped Amy to achieve success?

2. What sports stars do you know with health or physical problems? How have they overcome their problems?

3. Do you think that if you work hard and believe in something, you will get it? Give an example of someone who did just that.

4. Think of someone famous. Do not say his or her name. Tell your partner or the class about this person's life. Can they guess who it is?

Telling About Someone's Life

Writing in Present or Past Tense

Read the following facts about Amy Van Dyken.

The Story of Amy Van Dyken

1973	Amy is born in Englewood, Colorado. She is a sick child. The doctors tell her parents that she has asthma.
1991	Amy graduates from high school and goes to college.
1994	Amy is College Swimmer of the Year. She leaves college early. She wants to train for the Olympics.
1996	Amy is in the Olympics. She wins four gold medals. She is the first American woman to win four gold medals in the Olympics.
1998	Amy injures her shoulder.
1999	Amy wins one race, but she injures her shoulder again.
2000	Amy is in the Olympics. She wins two gold medals.

Exercise 1

Write the story of Amy Van Dyken in the past tense.

1973 <u>Amy was born in Englewood, Colorado. She was a sick child. The doctors told her parents that she had asthma.</u>

1991 _____

_____

1994 _____

_____

1996 _____

       _____

1998 _____

       _____

1998 _____

       _____

2000 _____

       _____

Now write the story of your life. Use the present tense or the past tense. The following models will help you:

I go (went) to high school/elementary school/college.
I graduate (graduated) from high school/college.

The Story of _____

19____   I was born in _____

       _____

       _____

19____   _____

       _____

       _____

19____   _____

       _____

       _____

19_____ _____
_____
_____

19_____ _____
_____
_____

19_____ _____
_____
_____

20_____ _____
_____
_____

Different Ways of Saying *when*

Read the following paragraph about Amy Van Dyken.

In 1973, Amy is born in Englewood, Colorado. She is a sick child. The doctors tell her parents that she has asthma. She starts to swim. When she is 13, she is a good swimmer. In 1991, Amy graduates from high school and goes to college. In 1994, she is College Swimmer of the Year. She leaves college early because she wants to train for the Olympics. In 1996, Amy goes to the Olympics and wins four gold medals. She is the first American woman to win four gold medals in one Olympics. In 1998, she injures her shoulder. In 1999, she wins one race, but she injures her shoulder again. In 2000, Amy wins two gold medals at the Olympics.

In the paragraph above, there are too many sentences that begin in the same way:

In 1973, . . .
In 1991, . . .
In 1994, . . .
In 1996, . . .

Underline the sentences in the paragraph above that begin this way. We can change some of them in the following ways:

In 1991, . . .   At age 18,
                    When she is 18,

In 1994, . . .   At age 21,
                    When she is 21,
                    Three years later,

In 1996, . . .   At age 23,
                    When she is 23,
                    Two years later,

In 1998, . . .   Two years later,
                    At age 25,
                    When she is 25,

In 1999, . . .   The next year,
                    One year later,
                    At age 26,

In 2000, . . .   The next year,
                    One year later,
                    The following year,

Look at the same paragraph about Amy Van Dyken. Use a different beginning in each of the blank spaces.

In 1973, Amy is born in Englewood, Colorado. She is a sick child. The doctors tell her parents that she has asthma. She starts to swim. When she is 13, she is a good swimmer. _____ Amy graduates from high school and goes to college. _____ she is College Swimmer of the Year. She leaves college early because she wants to train for the Olympics. _____ Amy goes to the Olympics and wins four gold medals. She is the first American woman to win four gold medals in one Olympics. _____ she injures her shoulder. _____ she wins one race, but she injures her shoulder again. _____ Amy wins two gold medals at the Olympics.

Exercise 4

Find the mistakes. There are 10 mistakes in grammar, punctuation, and capitalization. Find and correct them.

Amy Van Dyken was born in colorado, in the united states. Her parents are don and becky Van Dyken. Amy was the older of four children. She had two youngest brothers and a more younger sister. When she was still a baby the doctors found that she had Asthma.

Writing Practice

1. Rewrite in paragraph form.

    Step 1: Rewrite the sentences about your life (see pages 164–165) in the form of a paragraph.

    Step 2: Rewrite your paragraph again with only one "In 19___" at the beginning of a sentence. Use other words with the same meaning. Then check the checklist.

    Checklist
    _____ Did you indent the first line?
    _____ Did you give your paragraph a title?
    _____ Did you write the title with a capital letter?
    _____ Did you put the title in the center at the top of the page?
    _____ Did you write on every other line?

2. Edit your work.

    Work with a partner or your teacher to edit your sentences. Correct spelling, punctuation, vocabulary, and grammar.

3. Write your final copy.

Famous People Quiz

Name the person who . . .

1.   . . . **said**

> And so, my fellow Americans, ask not what your country can do for you; ask what you can do for your country.

. . . **was** president of the United States.

. . . **died in** 1963.

2.   . . . **said**

> I remain just one thing, and one thing only—and that is a clown.

. . . **was** a comedian.

. . . **made** silent movies.

. . . **was famous** for his hat and cane.

3.   . . . **said**

> If you want anything said, ask a man. If you want anything done, ask a woman.

. . . **was born** in England.

. . . **studied** at Oxford University.

. . . **became** prime minister of England in 1979.

Video Activity • An Interview with Tiger Woods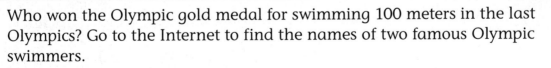

1. You are going to watch a video of Tiger Woods playing golf. Before watching it, discuss each of the following topics.

   - Place
   - Clothing
   - Sports equipment

   What do you expect to see in a game of golf? Write one or two key words for each topic. Then watch the video and check which of your key words appear in the video. Add words that you did not think of.

2. Watch the video again and listen to Tiger Woods as he says these sentences. Match the sentences that go together.

   ____ "You have to play well."   a. "You can always try again."

   ____ "If I don't win it this year, there's always next year."   b. "You go out there, it's a game and go play."

   ____ "It's not life or death."   c. "It's not easy."

3. What can you tell about Tiger Woods's personality from watching this video?

Internet Activity

Who won the Olympic gold medal for swimming 100 meters in the last Olympics? Go to the Internet to find the names of two famous Olympic swimmers.

Readings from Literature

CHAPTER FIFTEEN

A Poem

Pre-Reading Activity

Discuss these questions.

1. Describe what you see in the picture.
2. How do you feel when it rains?
3. What kind of weather do you like the most?
4. What kind of weather do you not like?

Key Vocabulary

Do you know these words? Match the words with the meanings.

1. ____ to beat
2. ____ to bounce
3. ____ to spill
4. ____ gutters
5. ____ to lick
6. ____ tin
7. ____ to bang

a. to rub the tongue over, as you do when you eat ice cream
b. to hit in a way that makes a sharp, loud noise
c. to hit again and again
d. a kind of metal
e. open pipes on a roof that catch and carry rain water
f. to hit so that the object (like a ball) comes back
g. to flow over

Rain
by Dionne Brand

It finally came,
it **beat** on the house
it **bounced** on the flowers
it **banged** on the **tin** roof
it rolled in the **gutters**
it made the street muddy
it **spilled** on the village
it **licked** all the windows
it jumped on the hill.
It stayed for two days
and then it left.

Vocabulary

Meaning

Complete the sentences with the words below.

bounced spilled
banged   beat
gutters   tin
licked

1. The rain made a loud noise when it hit the roof. It ——————— on the roof.

2. The roof was made of ———————.

3. The ——————— around the roof took the water from the roof to the street below.

4. The rain ——————— on the village, like water flowing out of a glass that was too full.

5. The rain hit the house over and over again. It ——————— on the house.

6. Like a ball hitting a wall, the rain ——————— on the flowers.

7. The rain, like a cat's tongue, ——————— the windows.

Vocabulary Activity

Choose the correct answer. Then use the answer in a complete sentence.

1. What object usually bounces?
   an apple   a ball   a flower

   Example: _A ball usually bounces._

2. What things do we usually lick?
   stamps   windows   flowers

3. Where do you see gutters?

   on a car   on a house   on a train

4. What do we beat?

   a drum   a chair   a book

5. What can bang?

   a cloud   a door   snow

Comprehension

Write complete answers to these questions.

1. What does "it" mean in the poem?

   _____

   _____

2. What kind of place do you think the poem describes?

   _____

   _____

3. How long did it rain?

   _____

   _____

4. Was it a light rain or a strong rain?

   _____

   _____

5. Were people waiting for the rain to come?

   _____

   _____

6. The rain in the poem is like an animal or a person. What animal do you think it can be? Why?

   _____

   _____

Discussion

Discuss these questions with your classmates.

1. Which words in the poem did you like most? Why? Which words did you dislike?

2. Draw a picture of the scene in the poem and show it to your classmates.

3. Read the poem aloud. Decide which words to say more loudly. What effect do you think this has?

Review of Parts of Speech

A *noun* is a word that names a person, place, or thing.

Examples:

man   Mexico   school

A *verb* is a word that describes an action or a state. Every sentence has a verb. Verbs change forms depending on tense and number.

Examples:

teach, taught   look, looked   I see, he sees

An *adjective* describes a noun or a pronoun.

Examples:

a **hot** day   **wet** streets   a **dark** sky

An *adverb* describes a verb, an adjective, or another adverb.

Examples:

The sun shines **brightly.**
The snow fell **gently.**

Exercise 1

Circle the correct answer.

1. Which is a noun?
    dark   snowed   sky

2. Which is a noun?
    covered   flowers   bright

3. Which is a noun?

   gentle   wet   snowstorm

4. Which is a verb?

   burned   hot   noisily

5. Which is a verb?

   light   softly   blew

6. Which is a verb?

   fast   whistled   rainy

7. Which is an adjective?

   cold   storm   shone

8. Which is an adjective?

   blizzard   sunny   froze

9. Which is an adjective?

   poured   strongly   skinny

10. Which is an adverb?

    cloudy   noisily   dry

11. Which is an adverb?

    violently   whispered   roared

12. Which is an adverb?

    freezing   muddy   brilliantly

Exercise 2

Look at the four weather words below, and write three verbs, two adjectives, one adverb, and one prepositional phrase that go with each one.

Noun	Snow	Wind	Rain	Sun
Verb	to snow			
Verb				
Verb				
Adjective				
Adjective				
Adverb				
Prepositional phrase				

Writing Practice

How to Write a Poem About Weather

Use the words in Exercise 2 to create your own weather poem. Read the instructions and look at the example.

Instructions	Example
Write a weather noun on the 1st line.	Snow
Write two adjectives on the 2nd line.	Soft, white
Write two *-ing* verbs on the 3rd line.	Falling, covering
Write an adverb and a prepositional phrase on the 4th line.	Gently through the night
Write the noun from the 1st line again.	Snow

CHAPTER SIXTEEN

A Fable

Pre-Reading Activity

Discuss these questions.

1. Fables are stories that give a message about life. Every country has fables. Do you know any?

2. Proverbs are one or two sentences that give a message about life.

   Example: The grass is always greener on the other side of the fence.

   Which do you prefer—proverbs or fables?

Key Vocabulary

Do you know these words? Match the words with the meanings.

1. ＿＿ to quarrel   a. to open up or untie

2. ＿＿ to determine   b. to persuade someone

3. ＿＿ to fetch   c. to argue or fight with words

4. ＿＿ a bundle of   d. together

5. ＿＿ to convince   e. to decide

6. ＿＿ united   f. to go and get

7. ＿＿ to undo   g. a bunch or group of

Father and Sons

Note: This reading is one of Aesop's fables. Aesop was an African slave. He went to Greece around the year 600 B.C. (before Christ) and wrote 350 stories for adults that teach a lesson about life.

A certain man had several sons who were always **quarreling** with each other. However hard he tried, he could not get them to live together in peace. So he **determined** to **convince** them of their stupidity in the following way. He told them to **fetch a bundle of** sticks and asked each son in turn to break it across his knee. All tried and failed. Then he **undid** the bundle, and gave them the sticks one by one. They had no difficulty breaking them. "There, my boys," he said. "**United** you will have power. But if you quarrel and separate, you will be weak."

Vocabulary

Meaning

Complete the sentences with the words below.

a bundle of   convinced
fetch   united
determined   quarreled
undid

1. The sons never agreed with one another. They ——————.

2. The father —————— to make his sons work together and be happy together.

3. The father —————— his sons that what they were doing was not good.

4. He told them to —————— some sticks.

5. The sons could not break —————— sticks.

6. The father —————— the bundle of sticks and gave each son one.

7. The father told his sons that —————— they will be strong.

Vocabulary Activity

Answer the questions. Use complete sentences.

1. Who often tells you to fetch something?

    Example: _My grandmother often tells me to fetch her glasses._

    ————————————————————————————————

    ————————————————————————————————

2. With what people did you quarrel recently?

    ————————————————————————————————

    ————————————————————————————————

3. What are you determined to do in the future?

   _____

   _____

4. Who convinces you to work hard at school?

   _____

   _____

5. What do you have a bundle of?

   _____

   _____

6. On what piece of clothing do you undo buttons?

   _____

   _____

Comprehension

Write complete answers to these questions.

1. How many sons did the man have?

    _____

    _____

2. What problem did the sons have?

    _____

    _____

3. What did the father tell them to do?

    _____

    _____

4. What did the sons try to do?

    _____

    _____

5. What happened?

    _____

    _____

6. What was the father's advice?

    _____

    _____

7. What is the meaning of the story? Circle the correct answer.
    a. You are stronger when you work alone.
    b. You are stronger together.
    c. Argument is bad.

Discussion

Discuss these questions with your classmates.

1. Can a parent give good advice?
2. Why is it sometimes difficult to work in a team?
3. What kind of person works well in a team?

Paraphrasing

When you paraphrase a sentence, you say the same thing in your own words. It is useful to look in a dictionary of synonyms or a thesaurus to find a different word with the same meaning.

Example:

Sentence: However hard he tried, he could not get his sons to live together in peace.

Paraphrase: He tried very hard, but he could not make his sons live with each other without fighting.

Exercise 1

Paraphrase these lines from the reading by replacing the underlined words. (Look back at the key vocabulary if you need help.)

1. So he determined to convince them of their stupidity.

   _____

   _____

2. He told them to fetch a bundle of sticks.

   _____

   _____

3. United you will have power.

   _____

   _____

4. If you <u>quarrel</u> and separate, you will <u>be weak.</u>

_____

_____

Every proverb has a meaning. Rewrite the proverb in your own words.

1. Proverb: In many words, a lie or two may escape.

   Rewrite: <u>When I talk too much, I may tell a lie.</u>

2. Proverb: You scratch my back and I'll scratch yours.

   Rewrite: _____

   _____

3. Proverb: Look before you leap.

   Rewrite: _____

   _____

4. Proverb: Actions speak louder than words.

   Rewrite: _____

   _____

5. Proverb: Children are a poor man's wealth.

   Rewrite: _____

   _____

When you are finished, show your sentences to your partner and compare your answers.

Find the mistakes. There are 10 mistakes in grammar, punctuation, and capitalization. Find and correct them.

We do not know two much about Aesop because he lived a long time ago. He lived to africa. He was not a freely man; he was slave. Later, he became a freely man and went to greece. There, he worked for the King as an ambassador. When he worked for the King some people got angry at him and killed him. But Aesop did not do anything wrong. Later, they made a Statue of Aesop in greece to remember him.

Writing Practice

Work alone, in pairs, or in groups. Write three proverbs from your country. Then rewrite each proverb in your own words.

Do you know these interesting facts about books?

Circle T if the answer is true. Circle F if the answer is false.

1. Charles Dickens wrote *Hamlet*.   T   F
2. Pavarotti is a famous Italian writer.   T   F
3. Shakespeare wrote plays.   T   F
4. Harry Potter is a character in a famous American
   children's book.   T   F
5. Agatha Christie wrote *Oliver Twist*.   T   F
6. The Bible has sold more copies than any other book.   T   F

Video Activity • Hurricane Season

CNN

1. You are going to watch a video about hurricanes. What do you know about hurricanes? What do you expect to see?

2. Watch the video. As you watch, write words to describe each of the following. Write a verb and an adjective for each noun.

	-ing Verb	Adjective
Waves	crashing	powerful
Trees		
Wind		
Rain		

3. Use your words to make a poem about hurricanes.

Internet Activity

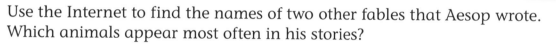

Use the Internet to find the names of two other fables that Aesop wrote. Which animals appear most often in his stories?

Answer Key

Unit 1: Do you know these interesting facts about special days?
1. T   2. T   3. F   4. F   5. T   6. F   7. F   8. T

Unit 2: Do you know these interesting facts about places?
1. c   2. b   3. a   4. b   5. a   6. c

Unit 3: Do you know these interesting facts about your body?
1. T   2. F   3. T   4. T   5. F   6. F

Unit 4: Do you know these interesting facts about customs?
1. T   2. F   3. F   4. T   5. T   6. F   7. T

Unit 5: Food Quiz
1. ginger ale / Ireland   2. chewing gum / Mexico
3. hot dog / United States   4. spaghetti / China
5. croissant / Austria   6. hamburger / Germany

Unit 6: Inventions Quiz
1. c   2. b   3. a   4. c   5. a. Germany   b. Mexico
c. China   d. Saudi Arabia   e. Brazil

Unit 7: Famous People Quiz
1. John F. Kennedy   2. Charlie Chaplin
3. Margaret Thatcher

Unit 8: Do you know these interesting facts about books?
1. F   2. F   3. T   4. F   5. F   6. T

Skills Index

Grammar and Usage

Adjectives, 19, 34–36, 140–142, 178, 179, 180, 181
  Comparative form, 44–46
  Superlative form, 46–48

Adverbs, 69–72, 178, 179, 180, 181
  too or *very*, 140–142
  when, 60–61

Comparison
  as . . . as for, 130–131
  Comparative form of adjectives, 44–46
  Superlative form of adjectives, 46–48

Complements, 19–20

Nouns, 8, 9, 19, 178–180, 181
  Count and noncount nouns, 82–85

Objects
  Objects of prepositions, 93
  Objects of verbs, 19, 20

Phrases
  Noun phrases, 8, 9, 19
  Prepositional phrases, 93–96

Prepositions
  Objects of prepositions, 93
  Prepositions of time, 155–156

Pronouns, 8, 9, 19
  it and *them*, 117–118

Question forms, 154–155, 157

Subjects, 8–9

Verbs, 9–10, 169, 178, 180, 181
  Linking, 19
  Objects of verbs, 19, 20
  Present or past tense, 163–167

when, 60–61

Word order, 8, 35

Listening/Speaking

Discussion, 7, 18, 33, 43, 59, 68, 81, 92, 105, 116, 129, 139, 153, 162, 176, 186

Listening to selections, 3, 14, 29, 40, 55, 65, 77, 89, 101, 112, 125, 136, 149, 159, 173, 183

Pre-reading activities, 2, 13, 28, 39, 54, 64, 76, 88, 100, 111, 124, 135, 148, 158, 172, 182

Reading

Chronological order, 163–165

Comprehension, 6–7, 17–18, 32–33, 42–43, 58, 67–68, 80, 91–92, 104, 114–115, 128, 138–139, 152–153, 161, 176, 187

Literary forms
  Biographies, 149, 159
  Fables, 183